Leningrad under Siege

Leningrad under Siege

First-hand Accounts of the Ordeal

by

Ales' Adamovich & Daniil Granin

Translated by
Dr Clare Burstall & Dr Vladimir Kisselnikov

Pen & Sword
MILITARY

First published in Great Britain in 2007 by
Pen & Sword Military
an imprint of
Pen & Sword Books Ltd
47 Church Street
Barnsley
South Yorkshire
S70 2AS

A CIP catalogue record for this book is
available from the British Library.

Typeset in Sabon and Bernhard Modern by
Lamorna Publishing Services

Printed and bound in England by Biddles Ltd

For a complete list of Pen & Sword titles please contact
PEN & SWORD BOOKS LIMITED
47 Church Street, Barnsley, South Yorkshire, S70 2AS, England
E-mail: enquiries@pen-and-sword.co.uk
Website: www.pen-and-sword.co.uk

Contents

Translators' Foreword

Many books have been written about sieges that happened in various places, in different times, in the course of numerous wars. At first glance this book might look, to the English-speaking reader, like just another book about one of these events, but the siege of Leningrad between 1941 and 1944 was one of the most crucial events of the Second World War. This is not the first book to be written on the subject but we believe it to be one of the most convincing and trustworthy because it is built on the basis of the thoughts, feelings and emotions of the people, who were either there or very close to it. The book includes diaries and interviews of men and women, young and old, belonging to different social classes but whose fate it was to live through the horrors and hardships of the siege.

One of us translators was born in November 1941 in the city of Sverdlovsk in the Urals, where his mother had been evacuated in July 1941. His grandfather died from starvation in the besieged city in April 1942 having just learned that he had a new grandson (it had taken more than four months for the telegram from Sverdlovsk to reach him). So neither of us is a '*blockadnik*' (the word used for marking those who stayed in Leningrad during the siege). But it was a hard job for us to read, re-read and translate these heart-rending pieces of evidence. Due to some practical publishing considerations we are presenting here only one of the two parts of the source book.

We would like to take this opportunity to express our gratitude to the people without whose kind and enthusiastic assistance and support this version of the book would not have been possible: N.

vii

Dobrotvorsky Senior Research Fellow at the State Memorial Museum of Defence and Siege of Leningrad; V. David, historian and writer and V. Golikov and E. Filippenko, computer experts. It goes without saying that we are grateful to Daniil Granin who unhesitatingly gave us his permission to make this English language version of his book.

We believe that it would be reasonable to introduce the reader to, or remind him of, the most meaningful events taking place before, during and after the siege of Leningrad.

The city of St Petersburg, which was renamed Leningrad in 1924, was founded in 1703 by Peter the Great in the swampy delta of the river Neva, as a 'window to Europe'. After having been the capital of the vast Russian Empire for about 200 years, it ceased to be the capital when the Bolshevik government moved it to Moscow. Following Lenin's death in 1924 it was renamed and became enshrined in communist lore as the cradle of the Great October Revolution (one of the reasons for Hitler's hatred of the city).

Leningrad's geographical location made it vulnerable to attack. In 1939 the Finnish frontier was within fifteen miles of the city's northern limits, with Estonia some 100 miles to the south-west. About forty miles to the east was Lake Ladoga, one of the largest lakes in Europe. Moscow was 450 miles away by rail. Finland and the Baltic states could easily have become a springboard for a German attack, the naval base and fortress of Kronstadt not being adequate protection against a landing from the Gulf of Finland, west of the city. So, the authorities in Moscow asked Finland to move the frontier to the Karelian Isthmus, forty-three miles further away from Leningrad in exchange for some other Russian territories. The Finnish government, however, refused to make any territorial concessions.

In August 1939 a Russo-German non-aggression pact was signed and, in October 1939, the Baltic states agreed to the stationing of Soviet troops in their territories. On 30 November 1939 the Red Army attacked Finland. The 'Winter War' proved to be far more prolonged and costly than Stalin had expected but, after nearly four months of stubborn resistance, Finland was forced to yield in March 1940. The Soviet Union received all that it had demanded and more, including a thirty-year lease of the Hango peninsula, a number of islands in the Gulf of Finland, the entire Karelian Isthmus with the town of Vyborg, and the northern shores of Lake Ladoga.

After the fall of France, the Soviet Union annexed the Baltic states in July 1940, thereby largely restoring the Russian frontiers of 1914. Leningrad was now a considerable distance from the frontier, while Soviet bases in the Baltic states guarded its sea approaches. In April 1941 moves were made to improve Leningrad's civil defence, providing for the construction of shelters and the strengthening of the civil defence organization, but war broke out before these moves could be fully implemented, leaving Leningrad inadequately prepared to deal with the expected air attacks. Little was done to improve the supply system or to increase the stocks of food and fuel in the city. According to the Soviet archives, on 21 June 1941 Leningrad had sufficient food reserves for little more than a month. On the eve of the German attack, the city's stockpile of coal and other fuels was sufficient only for normal peacetime needs. Official propaganda stressed the friendly relations between Germany and the USSR and branded any rumour to the contrary as a Western plot to sow discord between two friendly powers.

The early fall of France in the summer of 1940 came as a shock, leading to the mobilization of Soviet armed forces and their concentration on the frontiers. The German victories in the west showed the German army to be the most powerful in the world. After the fall of France, Hitler revived his anti-communist mission and decided to prepare for an attack on the USSR. Secret planning for the campaign began immediately. By 5 December the German army chiefs were ready to submit their plan to Hitler. It called for an advance into the Soviet Union by three army groups: a northern one aimed at Leningrad, a central one at Smolensk and Moscow, and a southern one at Kiev. Soviet military forces near the border and in the Baltic states were to be enveloped and destroyed. Hitler was particularly bent on the destruction of Leningrad and Stalingrad – 'the breeding places of Bolshevism'.

He adjusted the plan by giving first priority to the capture of Leningrad and Kronstadt and the destruction of the Russian forces in the Baltic States. There was to be no advance on

Moscow until these three objectives had been achieved. The codename for the plan was Operation Barbarossa. The plan called for Finland to assist Army Group North in the capture of Leningrad, but nothing had been done to secure a Finnish agreement.

At 3 a.m. on 22 June 1941, without any warning, the guns of the invading German armies opened fire and the troops began their advance. The Russian forces were caught by surprise along the entire front and were, at first, unable to offer any coordinated resistance. The *Luftwaffe* caught the Soviet air force on the ground and destroyed a major part of it.

Although the Red Army was slow to react to the German attacks, which Stalin had not anticipated, it was quickly active on the Finnish border. Three hours after the beginning of the German offensive, Soviet planes attacked Finnish warships and Red Army artillery opened fire along the frontier. Further Soviet military operations and air attacks on Finnish cities, including Helsinki, forced the Finns to declare war on 25 June.

Meanwhile Army Group North, along with the rest of the German Forces, was rapidly advancing. By 26 June, the Germans had reached the Dvina and captured Kovno, Riga, Yelgava and, three days later, the port of Liepaya and between twelve and fifteen Red Army divisions were destroyed. On Hitler's orders, Army Group North then halted to regroup. It renewed its offensive on 2 July and, by 8 July, had broken through the Pskov defences and captured Pskov and Opochka. It also penetrated deep into Estonia. Thus, in the first sixteen days of their offensive, the German armies had reached a position from which they could launch the attack on Leningrad.

The Soviet command hoped to form a new defence line in the Luga area, where thousands of Leningraders had been sent to build fortifications. The German advance slowed and became a series of frontal assaults against a stubborn enemy. The Germans turned west to bypass the main defences and crossed the Luga on 15 July. They were now in a position to make a quick thrust at Leningrad, but the German High Command, despite the pleas of the tank officers, chose instead to halt the advance, regroup, and spend the next three weeks improving the roads.

On 8 July, Hitler noted in his diary his intention to raze

Moscow and Leningrad to the ground and make them uninhabitable. This was to be done by the *Luftwaffe*. On 15 July Army Group North was told that its immediate mission was not to capture Leningrad, but to encircle it.

In mid-August the Germans took Kingisepp and Narva, Novgorod and Chudovo. The Soviet Forces defending the Luga line were slowly pushed back.

On the Karelian Isthmus a Finnish offensive rapidly forged ahead and by 21 July the Finns had reached Salmi at the old frontier on the northern shore of Lake Ladoga. By 16 August they had encircled Vyborg, captured Hiitola, and advanced some sixty-two miles along the western shore of Lake Ladoga.

At noon on 22 June, some nine hours after the start of the German attack, Molotov spoke on the radio to inform the people that the Soviet Union was at war. Stalin did not the address the nation until 3 July.

In Leningrad, as a precautionary measure, civil defence units were ordered to man their posts by 7 a.m. and all apartment house caretakers were ordered to stand guard with their gas masks at the entrances to their buildings.

When the news came, it left everyone stunned. Mobilization and martial law were declared in Leningrad and elsewhere.

A considerable number of schools were requisitioned for use as hospitals. Medical aid stations were placed on round-the-clock duty, blackout and civil defence instructions were broadcast by radio. There followed several days of relative quiet, restaurants and places of public entertainment remaining open.

The entire population of Leningrad was mobilized for defence work. All men between the ages of 16-50 and women between 16-45 had to work for three hours a day after finishing their normal jobs. The unemployed were expected to work eight hours a day. The only exceptions to this were defence workers, the sick, pregnant women and women with young children. Initially the civilian population dug slit-trenches and built bomb shelters, sandbagged vital buildings and valuable statues. The work was at first poorly organized and confused.

After the fall of Pskov on 8 July, the picture changed radically – they were used to build fortification belts at various distances from Leningrad. This effort was to last for three months, gaining momentum as the advance on the city grew. It involved not just hours, but days and weeks of labour away from Leningrad. The age range was extended on 9 August to 15-55 for men and 16-50 for women.

The mobilized labourers assembled at assigned places in the city in groups. Each labour column of several thousand was then transported, or marched, to the construction site. Assignments were usually to build tank traps, trenches, or fortified positions. Most of the people lacked proper working clothes or shoes.

The speed with which the extensive fortification belts were growing up around Leningrad, built by a population working with primitive hand tools and sometimes under fire, testifies to the industry of the workers.

On 23 July it was decreed that nearly 10,000 fire fighting teams should be set up in factories and apartment houses. On 27 July a 24-hour watch was ordered on old buildings along with a blackout of the city. Unnecessary items were to be removed from attics, the floors covered with sand, and barrels of water and boxes of sand were to be placed ready to extinguish incendiary bombs and fires. Self-defence groups involving the adult population between 16-60 were to be given compulsory training in civil defence techniques and children between 8 and 16 were also to be trained. These covered all apartment houses, factories, office buildings and institutions. A round-the-clock watch was to be maintained on the roofs and in the attics of all buildings. Larger housing units had their own medical and first-aid units. Each group of self defence workers usually had helmets, axes, crowbars, shovels, buckets, extinguishers or stirrup pumps, hoses and sand.

Large-scale work in bomb shelters began in July, and numerous slit trenches, and sometimes large dugouts, were dug in parks, gardens and around factories. A large number of hotels, schools, and public buildings were requisitioned as hospitals. Some gas shells were captured from Army Group North in July. This led to a decision to provide the population of Leningrad with gas masks.

Public buildings and monuments were protected by sandbags and a few, such as the Smolny Institute, were extensively camouflaged with netting. Windows were covered with strips of adhesive paper.

Air defence was provided by fighter planes, anti-aircraft guns and barrage balloons. Light guns were sometimes mounted on the roofs of large buildings. Anti-aircraft fire was supplemented by fire from the guns of ships in the harbour and on the Neva.

The alerts were announced via the radio loudspeakers, and the sounding of all available sirens and factory whistles. During the alerts everyone not on duty was ordered into the shelters. At night, however, many people were reluctant to go, especially if there was no shelter in their own building.

In August a system called 'barrack conditions' was introduced. It prohibited a part of the labour force from leaving factory premises at night. The workers, thus restricted, were permitted to go home once a week to visit their families. The measure was not unpopular since the workers benefited from the additional rest and the food in the canteens.

Industrial evacuation began in July 1941. As the Germans came closer to Leningrad, an increasing number of factories were ordered to pack up and leave for new locations in the east (Siberia and the Urals). The evacuation was only partially successful because of the difficulty of moving huge quantities of heavy machinery by rail. A factory shop was usually evacuated as a unit, taking its best and newest machinery.

By July the Germans and Finns had cut all major rail lines leading from Leningrad except the one to Moscow. This one line rapidly became overloaded with military traffic. By mid-August it was cut during the German advance on Mga. Much of the machinery, packed and ready to leave Leningrad, was trapped in the city when the siege began. Over 2,000 goods wagon loads were abandoned in the station yards and the machinery in the open wagons began to rust and deteriorate. Much of it was later moved east in the spring of 1942.

At the end of June the Leningrad authorities decided to evacuate nearly 400,000 children from the city and send them to rural districts in the Leningrad, Kalinin and Yaroslavl regions. They were sent with whatever school, nursery, orphanage or children's home they belonged to. On 29 June the first ten trains, carrying more than 15,000 children, left Leningrad for the countryside, some in the direction of the advancing Germans, to Pskov and Novgorod. The German advance and the bombing of the railways, killing some children, forced the authorities to bring many of them back. After a while the children were reassembled and evacuated further east, to the Kirov or Sverdlovsk regions or beyond. For a variety of reasons many children remained in the city.

Unemployed people, women and old people were authorized to leave on a voluntary basis. By 10 August nearly 500,000 people had been evacuated. On that date it was decided to evacuate an additional 400,000 women and children up to the age of fourteen. Less than a week later the growing danger to Leningrad forced the authorities to raise this number to 700,000, to be evacuated at the rate of 30,000 daily. The German advance prevented this evacuation from being completed. The evacuation was far from smooth and became increasingly chaotic. Authorization had to be obtained from local commissions. There was much confusion, because in many cases heads of families were evacuated separately from their wives and children, and children were sometimes separated from their parents altogether.

Sometimes the evacuees had to wait days at the Leningrad railway stations before their train left. Or they were left stranded en route, either because their train was requisitioned by the military or by traffic jams or damage to the rails. Food and water was a problem. The majority of the population was torn between fear of staying and fear of leaving. Letters from refugees told of the hardships involved and people hated abandoning their hard-won possessions and breaking up their families. The German attacks on evacuation trains caused a lot of fear.

When the Germans approached the city, all private phones were disconnected – it became very difficult for people to keep in touch with one another. They were exposed to Soviet propaganda and also waves of rumours. Only the Soviet Information Bureau was authorized to issue daily news communiqués. These were very vague about the extent of the German advance. In general, the fighting was described as taking place 'in the direction of' a certain city, while the loss of that city was either not announced at all, or reported only after great delays. The fighting 'in the direction of Pskov' was not reported until 12 July although the city had actually been taken by the Germans on 8 July. Pskov continued to be reported as a battleground until 24 July, after which references ceased.

In July and early August there was little in the official news that would have alerted the people of Leningrad to the fact that their city was seriously threatened by the Germans. The greater the efforts of the authorities to hide the truth, the more widespread became the popular reliance on word-of-mouth information.

Having reached the area of Krasnogvardeisk, some seventeen miles south of Leningrad on 19 August, the Germans stopped their direct advance on the city. The Eighth Panzer Division, which had spearheaded this advance, turned back south to attack from the rear the large Soviet forces that were still defending the Luga River line. The rest of August was spent in the encirclement and destruction of these forces.

The Eighteenth Army took Tallin on 28 August after long heavy fighting. The Red Army elements involved were evacuated by sea to Leningrad in an operation that cost the Soviet navy numerous warships and transports. To the north of Lake Ilmen the Germans attacked from Chudovo along the railway and highway in the direction of Leningrad, while another unit advanced north towards the railway station at Mga on the Leningrad-Moscow railway line, the last open line to the Soviet capital. They succeeded in crossing the Izhora River by the end of August, but encountered the fortified belt that had been built by the Leningraders between Ust-Tosno and the Izhora River, and were unable to expand the bridgehead. To the north-east the Germans cut the Leningrad-Ovinichi railway line and, by 30 August, had advanced to the area of Mga as well as the Neva River at Ivanovskoye. Thus the fortification belt guarding Leningrad from the Gulf of Finland to the Neva River east of Kolpino was reached along a considerable part of its length, while the east railway line connecting Leningrad with the outside was cut at Mga.

During this time the Finns had been developing their offensive on the Karelian Isthmus. The attack on Vyborg began on 22 August and, on 25 August, the Finns cut the Vyborg-Leningrad railway line. On 29 August they entered Vyborg and two days later they reached the 1939 Russo-Finnish border at Mainila. They took Koivisto and a few days later the Soviet forces in the eastern part of the isthmus also withdrew to the pre-1939 frontier.

The stage was thus set for the final assault on the city. But on 21 August Hitler issued an order that gave top priority to the seizure of the Ukraine and the Crimea and to the encirclement of Leningrad by combined German-Finnish forces. The successful encirclement of Leningrad required close cooperation with the Finns and a considerable Finnish advance below the old frontier on the Karelian Isthmus. But Mannerheim wanted only to move his forces a short distance beyond the frontier to the narrowest part of the Karelian Isthmus, where he planned to establish a defence line. As a result, a substantial gap was to remain between the two armies, which left Leningrad with free access to Lake Ladoga.

On 8 September the Germans took Schlüsselburg, thus eliminating Leningrad's last land link with the rest of the country. During the first ten days of September Leningrad was also subjected to its first artillery and air bombardments. Although the Red Army was making desperate attacks along the Volkhov River and fighting tenaciously for every foot of ground around the city, the Germans continued to battle their way through the fortifications. On 14 September the 41st Panzer Corps reached the Pulkovo Heights, beating back all Russian counter-attacks. Having crossed most of the fortified belt, the German tank forces were poised for the last dash into the city, which was now only about seven miles away. But at that moment they were ordered to halt at defensive positions in preparation for their withdrawal three days later to serve with Army Group Centre. Thus the fruits of their victory were denied to them at the very moment when they seemed within their grasp. The next day the Eighteenth Army completed its advance to Uritsk, thereby cutting off the Soviet forces along the Gulf of Finland between Kopore and Oranienbaum and approaching to within four miles of the outskirts of Leningrad. Two days later it completed the encirclement of Soviet forces around Oranienbaum. This pocket was to survive until January 1944.

Fighting continued until 25 September, marked by minor German advances and numerous fierce Soviet counter-attacks, aimed primarily at breaking the encirclement. The Germans took Detskoye Selo and Peterhof and reached Volkhovstroi, east of

Leningrad, not, however, without encountering fierce resistance everywhere. The crossing of the Neva River and meeting up with the Finns, however, was out of the question. Army Group North had no choice but to break off its attacks and revert to a defensive position along the line of the Leningrad Front. The troops began to dig in but, although anticipating a long siege, they were confident that starvation would drive the defenders of Leningrad to surrender. By withdrawing the armoured divisions just at the moment when the capture of the city seemed certain, Hitler had saved it.

In Leningrad measures were taken to deny the enemy the use of the city in the event of its capture. These included laying demolition charges under factories, bridges, port and railroad installations. The hundreds of bridges across the Neva and the canals were mined. Various buildings including factories were mined, so that they could be collapsed across important streets in order to form barriers to the German advance. These preparations were seriously hampered by the beginning of artillery and air bombardments of the city. By early September the Germans had advanced sufficiently close to Leningrad to bring the city under long-range artillery fire. The bombardment was to continue with varying degrees of intensity until January 1944. The first large air raid occurred on 8 September and did considerable damage. Following this the German air attacks increased in intensity.

The Germans deliberately spaced their attacks in order to interfere as much as possible with the activities of the population. The artillery bombardment on 15 September, for example, lasted for over eighteen hours. There could be as many as twelve air raid alerts in a day. The largest attacks occurred on 19 and 27 September.

The Germans concentrated their attacks on factories, food storage areas, electric power stations, waterworks, military installations and naval vessels, but they also hit many residential buildings. During the first weeks of the bombardment most people slept in the shelters or ran for cover every time they heard a German plane. But after a while people got used to the situation and took cover only when bombs and shells were falling nearby.

The Germans had launched an attack in the direction of Tikhvin on 26 October. They advanced slowly over difficult terrain and in the face of strong Russian resistance. On 9 November they finally captured Tikhvin. They also advanced to the vicinity of Volkhov and Voibokalo in the north and Malaia Vishera to the south. There, however, they were halted by the Fifth Army without being able to reach the shores of Lake Ladoga.

During the following month both sides engaged in heavy fighting for Tikhvin and the railway line west of it. The recapture of this city was essential for the Russians if Leningrad was to survive the winter. As long as Tikhvin remained in German hands, it was impossible to supply Leningrad with the food and material necessary to prevent its fall.

The Soviet offensive broke through the German positions on 4 December and forced the Germans to leave the city on 8 December. By mid-December the Russians managed to reopen the railway supply route to Lake Ladoga. Two weeks later the Germans had re-crossed the Volkhov River and were back in the positions they had held around Leningrad in September.

In Leningrad people began to hide the deaths of family members in order to use their ration cards until they expired. Consequently, the authorities were unable to keep an exact count of the deaths occurring in the city. Fear of losing their ration status was one of the factors that drove the Leningraders to work and kept them there until they collapsed or died. In addition to suffering starvation, people were tortured by cold. Their wasted bodies became acutely sensitive to the abnormally low temperatures of that winter. The collection and burial of corpses became a problem. People had to take their dead to the cemeteries or leave them in courtyards, from which corpses were later removed by truck for mass burial, without coffins. There was an ever-growing parade of carts and sleds transporting the dead through the main streets of Leningrad.

As fuel became more scarce, the freezing weather led to the breakdown of the water, sewage and central heating systems in homes. People began to buy or make small temporary stoves, called *burzhuiki*. These were made from cans, bricks, metal barrels, etc. They were usually placed on the floor or on a stool beneath a ventilation shaft, which served as a chimney. As a rule, they were used for both heating and cooking. Generally only one room in an apartment could be heated at all and then only for short periods. Everyone lived and slept in this one room. Even then the temperature could be kept barely above freezing. These stoves were often badly made and were the source of many fires which, owing to the water shortage, became quite large.

When the electric power failed, most Leningraders managed to make primitive oil lamps, often consisting simply of a tiny wick floating in a little oil or paraffin. Candles were in very short supply.

In view of the water shortage and the cold, many Leningraders stopped washing and shaving. Washing clothes was a luxury few indulged in.

Freezing weather and bomb damage made the sewage system inoperable. Garbage and excrement were either thrown into courtyards or streets or dumped in abandoned rooms. Fortunately it was so cold that these practices did not create a serious health hazard in the winter.

The accumulated snow and ice made the streets increasingly impassable. Although decrees were issued mobilizing the population for street-cleaning, the weakened people lacked the incentive to carry them out effectively and most streets accumulated a thick crust of snow and ice, which was not removed until spring.

The intense cold and the physical weakness of the Leningraders put a halt to most of the fire watches on the roofs of buildings. The civil defence teams disintegrated as more and more of their members fell ill, died or were evacuated, and many workers slept in their factories and offices instead of returning home.

People also began to disregard the civil defence regulations that made it mandatory to seek shelter during an alert. At night particularly, people preferred to stay in bed. The militia still tried to enforce the regulations, but they were often openly disobeyed.

From September to December 1941 the publication of the copies of the major Leningrad newspaper became sporadic or ceased. It became increasingly necessary to rely on newspapers posted on bulletin boards and in workshops and offices, or read aloud in air-raid shelters. The use of radios was curtailed by the lack of electric power. Only some of the public loudspeakers mounted in the streets continued to function and, in any case, people were increasingly disinclined to stay in the cold to listen.

From a military point of view December 1941 proved to be a turning point in the war on the eastern front. The German *Blitzkrieg* had collapsed with Hitler's failure to capture either Leningrad or Moscow and the weakened German forces had to bear the brunt of a general Soviet counter-offensive that came close to destroying the German invasion armies. The Germans were forced to carry out extensive and costly retreats. Army Group North held out better than the others, but it was forced to retreat from Tikhvin, thus giving up the possibility of carrying out a complete encirclement of Leningrad.

But the city itself was living through its most trying days. Shrouded in snow and ice, silent except for the noise of gunfire on the front, in the winter of 1941-42 it resembled a ghost town rather than a city still housing millions of people. All public transportation had ceased. The streets were empty of vehicles except for an occasional army lorry. Nearly every factory was at a standstill.

Yet the same month brought the first real ray of hope to the city. The Soviet counter-offensive had reduced the military threat to Leningrad. The ice road became firmly established and well enough organized to allow the city authorities to increase the level of food rationing and evacuate a substantial number of the non-combatant population. But the effect of the ice road could only be perceived slowly. It was a life and death race between the improvements that the road provided and the deterioration of the physical condition of the city and its inhabitants.

On New Year's Eve there was a special issue of supplies, chiefly alcohol, sweets and some fats, but for the vast majority of the population the rations remained below subsistence level for another month.

In the last two months of 1941 the overall military situation began to change in favour of the Soviet Union. The Soviet offensive at Stalingrad was launched on 19 November and was followed by other offensives in the northern Caucasus and in the Kursk area. These operations developed into a general Soviet winter offensive along the entire front, during which the German losses of both men and material were heavy and they were forced to retreat from many areas along the front.

The Soviet High Command also drew up new plans for

breaking the blockade of Leningrad and the Volkhov forces in the area immediately south of Lake Ladoga, where the German Eighteenth Army held a ten mile wide, heavily fortified strip of territory. The attack began on 12 January 1942. The Soviet units made slow but steady progress and on 18 January a meeting of the attacking armies was effected. At the same time the city of Schlüsselburg was taken. The German blockade was broken and a narrow corridor, between five and six miles wide, along the southern shore of Lake Ladoga, was occupied by the Soviet forces. But, despite great effort, the Red Army was unsuccessful in its attempt to lift the blockade of Leningrad completely. The city remained under German fire for another year. But the liberated corridor, though narrow and harassed by German artillery fire, permitted re-establishment of a direct rail line to Leningrad.

In March 1942 Leningrad began its slow recovery and managed to withstand a further year and a half of siege and every German attempt to destroy it. After mid-February, food and other supplies became increasingly available but improvements in living conditions came about very slowly. The death rate remained high, particularly throughout May. The bread ration instituted on 11 February remained in force throughout the remainder of the year. The major changes were in the quality of the bread and in the increasing availability of other staples. During the summer the available food reached its highest level, owing in part to the local cultivation of vegetables. School children were offered hot meals at their school, a measure which sharply increased attendance.

Electric power was reserved primarily for the use of industry, the transportation system, and essential utilities. Although additional electric power became available in the autumn of 1942, when Leningrad was reconnected to the Volkhov Hydroelectric Station, most Leningraders did not receive any electricity in their homes at all during 1942. One of the immediate results of the reopening of the power stations was the partial revival of the tramcar service.

The renewal of the German aerial bombardment in April 1942 and the increase in artillery attacks meant that the civil defence system had to be revived and reorganized, as much of it had ceased to function during the winter months. Despite the intensification of the artillery barrages, the renewal of air raids, and the reduced size of the population, the Germans failed to halt the city's gradual recovery. The heroic and tragic period of the siege had come to an end by August 1942. From that time, despite its frequent crises and constant dangers, life in Leningrad assumed a semblance of normality. Costly as it was for the defenders to hold out, the city was a thorn in the side of the Germans and pinned down forces vitally needed by the enemy to hold its crumbling fronts elsewhere in the Soviet Union.

With reinforcements from outside, the Soviet Forces had built up a substantial superiority over the Germans in both numbers and fire power. A major offensive was launched from the Oranienbaum area on 14 January 1943, in conjunction with attacks on the Volkhov and Novgorod fronts. The following day the Leningrad forces began an assault along the entire front after fierce fighting. The Red Army captured Krasnoye Selo on 19 January, then Pushkin, Mga, Gatchina and finally Krasnogvardeisk on 26 January. The Germans were forced to retreat all along the front, leaving behind the heavy artillery pieces with which they had bombarded Leningrad. On 27 January 1943, to the sound of twenty-four salvos from 324 guns, Zhdanov, the regional Party Secretary, and General Govorov, the Commander-in-Chief of the Leningrad Front, made the long-awaited announcement:

In the course of the fighting a task of historic importance has been achieved: the city of Leningrad has been completely freed from the enemy's blockade and from the enemy's barbarous artillery bombardment.

Dramatis Personae

Georgi Alexeievich Kniazev – diarist, historian and Director of the Archives of the Academy of Sciences in Leningrad.

Valya – a small girl that Georgi and his wife had intended to care for in their home.

Lidiya Georgievna Okhapkina – diarist and mother of two small children.

Vasili Ivanovich – Lidiya's husband.

Tolya – Lidiya's son.

Ninochka – Lidiya's daughter.

Yura Riabinkin – diarist and schoolboy.

Antonina Mikhailovna – Yura's mother.

Ira – Yura's sister.

Tina – Yura's aunt.

Anfissa Nikolaievna – Yura's neighbour.

Nina Alexandrovna Abkina – engineer and interviewee.

Alexandra Mikhailovna Arsenyeva – refugee and interviewee.

Yevgenia Porfirievna Ştroganova – daughter of Alexandra Mikhailovna Arsenyeva.

Daniil Granin – co-author of the book and interviewee.

Maria Vasilievna Motkovskaya – interviewee responsible for evacuees.

1

Three Out of Three Million

This book is mostly about three remarkable people, two men and a woman. They never met; never knew anything about one another. The first, Georgi Alexeievich Kniazev, was a historian; the second, Yura Riabinkin, was a fifteen year old boy at the outbreak of war; and the third, Lidiya Georgievna Okhapkina, was the mother of two small children.

During the siege, many Leningraders kept diaries. Others would just jot down some experience they had undergone, while it was still fresh in their minds. People sent or brought their notebooks to us, often old accounts books in which they had recorded what they had lived through, written in pencil or in faded ink, neatly or hastily, briefly or in detail, sometimes with a numbed hand. From all these diaries and notes we selected the three accounts that had made the deepest impression on us. Not a word has been added to them, nor any changes made: we allowed ourselves to do no more than shorten them, omitting repetitions and entries that had nothing to do with the events of the siege.

In St Petersburg (formerly Leningrad) memorial plaques tend to be distributed sparingly. There are simply too many places and buildings worthy of mention, of emphasis. This being so, there is a particular building on Vasilievsky Island that always attracts attention.

If you were to walk along the Neva embankment from the University towards the granite Sphinxes reclining above the waters of the Neva near the former Academy of Arts building – nowadays the Repin Institute – then immediately after the Sphinxes a three-storey building with a portico supported by four

Doric columns would come into view. It is a building in the old-fashioned style – nice, unassuming, typically Petersburg architecture – renovated in 1806-1808 by the famous architect Zakharov. Its walls are hung all over with cast-iron memorial plaques. There is no other residential building in St Petersburg, nor in Moscow either – for that matter, probably nowhere else in the world – that has so many memorial plaques: it has twenty-seven of them. The building belongs to the Academy of Sciences and was home to many eminent Russian scholars and scientists: the philologist Yakov Karlovich Grot, for example; the Byzantine scholar Fyodor Ivanovich Uspensky; the physicist Boris Semyonovich Yakobi; Vasili Vladimirovich Petrov, the first Russian electro technical engineer and Ivan Petrovich Pavlov, who lived there until his death in 1936. Whichever name you pick from the twenty-seven that are commemorated there, a whole branch of science opens up.

And it was in this building, which had become, to some extent, a symbol of Russian scientific endeavour, that Georgi Alexeievich Kniazev, the Director of the Archives of the Academy of Sciences, was living when war broke out. He could just as well have lived out his life in some other building and in it written his papers on the history of the Academy of Sciences and on aspects of archiving, but the fact that he lived in that particular building throughout the siege and that it was there that he wrote his diary – *A Half-Century in the Life of a Middle-Ranking Russian Intellectual* – takes on an unexpected significance.

Georgi Alexeievich Kniazev's legs were partially paralyzed. He had difficulty walking and travelled from his home to work and back in a wheelchair. It was rare for him to undertake longer journeys. The Archives of the Academy of Sciences were situated on the same embankment, beyond the University, within the Academy building, about 800 metres from Kniazev's home. In essence, that stretch of pavement along the embankment was Kniazev's main road during the whole of the siege; the little segment of the city that was in his field of vision became the narrow backdrop against which the war unfolded for him: the siege, the shelling, the air raids, the famine, the evacuations.

Turning now to his diary:

23 June 1941. The 2nd day of the war. I never did manage to find out the details about the opening of Timur's tomb. Military events pushed the information about the archaeological excavations in Samarkand into the background.

How everything in this world repeats itself! In the fourteenth century, Timur, or Tamberlane, conquered India from the Ind to the Ganges, and Persia, Syria, Turkey and southern Russia.

And now here comes another one – the upstart Hitler – who has gone far beyond Timur the Lame in bringing so much suffering both to his own people and to all other peoples, to the enslaved and the humiliated as well as to those fighting against his hellish regime.

The first of the wounded have been brought into Leningrad. The new Mannerheim Line beyond Vyborg has been broken through in several places by our detachments. A German airborne force of several thousand men has also been wiped out.

The second day of the Great Patriotic War has come to an end. It has exhausted me. The blood is throbbing in my head and there seems to be the sound of propellers droning in my ears all the time.

25 June 1941. The 4th day. This morning, after all the windows had been pasted over with strips of white adhesive paper, some woman arrived and said that in their establishment they had been ordered to glue on black strips, not white ones... Be that as it may, all the windows in the buildings are plastered with strips of white paper.

We are following the situation at the Front on the map. Intensive, awful fighting. The question that troubles us most is what will happen if the Germans manage to cut the Kirovsk-Murmansk railway line. There are particularly violent battles taking place in the area around Kandalaksha.

At work I held discussions with representatives of the special archive collections. In a number of cases we decided not to transfer the most precious materials to the damp basements which are prone to flooding...

What do you see from your window, on your way to work? Birch trees? A river? Houses? For Georgi Alexeievich Kniazev it was the Sphinxes. As though it had been arranged specially for him – he being a historian. But also because he collected and noted down facts that pointed to the progress or otherwise of the human race. The ancient Sphinxes were always within his field of view.

They lie there, made of rose-coloured stone, almost the same colour as the granite embankments, with their human faces and animal paws, opposite one another, and the old inscription tells how the Sphinxes from Ancient Thebes in Egypt were transported to the city of Saint Peter in 1832. They seem so much at home there – witnesses to an already lengthy history of the endless 'soaring and falling of mankind along the road to progress', as Kniazev puts it.

The diary again:

The two bronze lanterns that used to stand near the Sphinxes have been dismantled and taken away. The Sphinxes are still there... I was looking at them today with deep emotion, but I wasn't able to turn it into a poem.

Just the same, here I sit, writing these notes. Why? Because I can't help but write. But I am not going to chase after what is beyond me. My notes will be confined to what goes on within my own 'small world'. Who am I writing for? For you, my faraway friend, a member of some future Communist society, to whom war will seem as alien and fundamentally repugnant as cannibalism now seems to us. Yet there once were people, our ancestors, who happily devoured one another! I do believe – and in this respect I am an incorrigible optimist – that a time will come when there will be no war on earth.

That is why I am writing my notes, come what may. And I am not put off by the thought that they might well perish, might go up in flames in some dreadful moment of a future bombing raid on our city. Nor am I put off by the thought that I might perish too.

But if they do reach you, my faraway friend, these pages of mine – perhaps in scorched fragments – you will live through with me what your unfortunate predecessor lived through and held dear,

4

who was obliged to live in a 'prehistoric' era, but also at the dawning of the true history of the human race. In the official documents that will have been preserved for you, you will find the materials for a scientific treatise, but in my notes you will find the beating pulse of the life of one insignificant man who, within his own small world, lived out a life that was big, boundless, complex, tragic and full of contradictions.

In the courtyard, in the little garden, there has been a gathering of the residents of the building. My wife was there too. Any minute now she will come and tell me what was going on down there.

Ten-thirty in the evening. The latest news on the radio. Turkey has declared her neutrality. A huge outburst of popular enthusiasm is sweeping the country in response to the onset of the Great Patriotic War.

The peoples of Europe must surely rise up!

26 June 1941. The 5th day. We slept peacefully through the night. There were no air-raid alerts. Which means that the noise I was hearing was inside my ears. It is interesting that I am not alone in experiencing this auditory illusion: others have observed it too.

At work it was a normal working day. I took some students on an excursion and delivered a lecture to them with great panache.

In the evening we read the regulations about how to behave and the measures to be undertaken in the event of an alert. My wife went along to the first-aid post. I sorted out our stock of medical supplies in case of burns or wounds.

28 June 1941. The 7th day. A nerve-racking, totally nerve-racking day. At work an extra unsettling element was introduced by one of my women colleagues. Affected by the threatening situation that had been announced and by the news about the evacuation of the children, she had evidently formed a grim conclusion about the state of affairs at the Front in connection with the infiltration of enemy tank divisions into the positions occupied by our troops at Minsk and elsewhere. This mood immediately infected others, especially those who had come in tired after a night of futile guard duty in the main building of the Academy of Sciences. As the colleagues who had been on duty there put it, they had been 'guarding the chairs in the president's office', while the Archives had been left unprotected. I did everything that I could to raise the mood.

During the morning all my colleagues were hauling sand up to the attic.

Yura Riabinkin introduces himself in his diary with the following brief autobiography:

I was born on 2 September 1925 in the city of Leningrad. I live with my mother, my sister and my aunt. My mother works at the centre housing the Regional Committee of the Industry and Building Trades Union, where she is in charge of the library. She has been a Party member since 1927. My aunt is a doctor and currently at the Front. My sister is eight years old. My father abandoned the family in April 1933, married again and went off to Karelia. Later on, so they say, in 1937, he was deported to the city of Ufa.

Until I was seven years old I was brought up at my aunt's place in the country.

In 1933 I started school and have now completed eight classes and been moved up into the ninth class.

In 1938-39 I also attended a marine study group in the Kuibyshevsky district and went to summer school in Strelna, where I earned my Young Seaman's badge. In addition, alongside my school work, I have also been a member of the history study group at the Pioneer Palace for the past three years. I have presented papers on Bagration, Suvorov, and other such topics, for which I got a 'Good'.

Yura Riabinkin

Like everyone else, Yura described the day war began in great detail. It was a day that everyone remembered.

22 June 1941. All night long some buzzing noise outside the window wouldn't let me get to sleep. When it finally died down a little towards morning, day was dawning. At this time of year in

Leningrad the nights are moonlit, light and short. But when I looked out of the window, I could see several searchlights probing the sky. I fell asleep just the same. It was gone ten in the morning when I woke up. I quickly put my clothes on, washed, had something to eat and made my way to the Pioneer Palace garden. I had made up my mind to get a qualification in chess this summer. One way or another I often win, even against qualified players.

Once I was out in the street, I noticed something peculiar. At the gateway to our building I caught sight of the caretaker with a gas mask and wearing a red armband on his sleeve. The same thing at all the other gateways. The militiamen had their gas masks with them and there was even a radio broadcasting at each of the crossroads. Something told me that a situation threatening the city had been declared.

When I got to the Palace, I found only two chess players there. It was probably too early. Indeed, a bit later on, several more people arrived. While I was setting the pieces out on the chessboard, I got wind of something new in the air and, turning round, I noticed a group of children clustering around one small boy. I pricked up my ears and was rooted to the spot...

'Yesterday at four in the morning German bombers carried out raids on Kiev, Zhitomir, Sevastopol and elsewhere,' the boy was saying excitedly. 'Molotov came on the radio. We are now at war with Germany!'

Well, I simply sank down, stunned. This was some news! And I hadn't even suspected anything of the kind! Germany! Germany has declared war on us! That's why they all had their gas masks.

My head was in a spin. I couldn't think straight. I played three games. Strange to relate, I won all three, then pushed off home. In the street I stopped by a loudspeaker and listened to Molotov's speech.

When I got home only Mother was there. She already knew what had happened.

After I'd had my dinner I went out into the street to have a walk around. You could feel a sort of tension everywhere – the whole stifling, dusty atmosphere of the city was full of it. On my way back home I joined a queue for a newspaper. The papers hadn't come yet, but there was a huge queue. Odd conversations were running through the queue; jokes with an international flavour and sceptical comments were doing the rounds.

'And what will happen if Germany and England conclude a peace treaty and they have a go at us together?'

'Now we will be bombing everything in sight, not like it was in Finland, even residential areas – let the proletariat start to use its voice, realize what it is getting into.'

'Did you hear that a German plane was shot down near Olgino?'

'Imagine it flying as far as that!'

'Yes, get ready for air raids. Just you wait till there are 300 of them flying over Leningrad!'

'There's no way to avoid it. Everything will happen in its turn.'

Having spent about two hours in the queue, I had just made up my mind to leave when they suddenly announced that, although there would be no newspapers, there would be some kind of official bulletin, but when this would be, no one knew. After hanging around for about half an hour more, I went home anyway. Nina, our domestic help, went out in search of a paper.

The day is coming to an end. Half-past eleven by the clock. A grave and definitive struggle has begun. Two opposing systems, socialism and fascism, have clashed! On the outcome of this great historical battle hangs the welfare of all mankind.

26 June 1941. Today, as soon as I got up, I went to the Palace. From there, together with the other lads, I went on to the construction site by the Kazan Cathedral. I worked from eleven in the morning till nine in the evening with a break for dinner. The break lasted an hour. Both my hands got calloused and had splinters in them. I lugged planks, dug holes in the ground, sawed and chopped wood – all sorts of things had to be done. Towards the end my arm began to ache so much that I couldn't saw any more. During the dinner break at home I started to read *Virgin Soil* by Turgenev. I returned home in the evening. Mother had come home early from her shift – she had been relieved. Well, I can't write much – I am running out of time. I have to go to the Palace.

28 June 1941. I worked at the Pioneer Palace again today on the construction of a bomb shelter. It was hellish hard work. Today we became stonemasons. My hands were completely wrecked by the hammer – they are all covered with scratches now. But we were relieved early – about three o'clock. So we worked for four hours and a half, but it was some work!

Leaving the Palace, I went to see Mother. She is in a very anxious state and goes around wrapped in gloom the whole time. The possibility of chemical warfare has been raised, and they are now beginning to evacuate people. I took five roubles and went to a public dining room. Then I went home. Some woman came who was making a list of all the children under thirteen. Ira's name was put on the list. The manager of our apartment block ordered Nina to be on watch by the gates from half-past nine in the evening until three in the morning. Incidentally, he informed us that, in the event of an alert, we were to run down to the Khamadulins', on the ground floor. All the same, it's not safe even there. You couldn't escape from a high-explosive bomb, nor from a shock wave either: the shock wave would bring the building down, and the rubble would bury us in the basement. Your chances of surviving a chemical bomb would be even less.

29 June 1941. I worked at the Palace on the construction of the bomb shelter. Before that I had been loading sand in Lassalle Square. But the work there was fairly minor. The lads traced Hitler's ugly mug in the sand and began bashing it with their shovels. I joined in as well.

At the Palace I lugged bricks and sand again. I left the Palace at six o'clock. When I got home, I received an unexpected surprise.

While I was still in the doorway, Ira came running up to me shouting: 'See what Mother has bought for me! And she didn't buy anything for you! Not anything!' I went into the dining room. On the sofa lay a sailor's smock and a doll that Mother had bought for Ira. On the table stood a pair of new boots for Ira.

9

Mother slipped some sort of a note into my hand. I unfolded it mechanically. It was an application to the Military Committee for Mother and me to join the ranks of the Red Army as volunteers. It turned out that there had been a Party meeting at Mother's place in the morning and all the Party members had decided to join the ranks of the Red Army. No one had refused. At first I felt a certain sense of pride, then a wave of fear – the first eventually got the upper hand of the second.

In the evening Mother and I went to see the owner of a house in Siverskaya. Mother had decided to send Ira and Nina there if we went off to the Front. One way or another they came to some agreement.

That same evening I went to the hairdresser's. It was probably about two months since I'd last had a haircut.

30 June 1941. When I got to the Palace, I found some lads playing billiards. I played for about half an hour, then we went to work on the bomb shelter. Once more I lugged sand from the garden. I was released around seven in the evening. I went to the recruitment information centre. They had some different news for me there – I probably won't be taken into the army: I am too young and, besides, I suffer from pleurisy. Given the fact that I am feeling poorly, and the pleurisy is really making itself felt, they will probably excuse me from working at the Palace and might send me to a Young Pioneers' camp.

Communication with Aunt Tina has been broken off. She can't come here, because she is registered in Schlüsselburg, and it would be too dangerous to go to her. At nine in the evening I went to visit Dodya Finkelstein. He isn't working anywhere – he is free. His little brother is to be sent to Malaya Vishera the day after tomorrow. I told him about the Palace. He decided he would come and work there too. I left his place around eleven o'clock.

The third main character in this book is Lidiya Georgievna Okhapkina. At that time she was twenty-eight years old. On the morning of 22 June 1941, she was getting ready to return to their dacha, where she and her children had been staying. Her husband, Vasili Ivanovich, was away on a job, and her nephew and a relative of her husband's, Shura Samsonov, had come to see Lidiya Georgievna off:

Everything had been packed by then and I was breast-feeding my daughter, who was then five months old. All of a sudden, 'Attention! Attention!' came over the radio and Molotov began to make his speech. I said that we wouldn't go to the dacha. We had to wait for my husband. I was not a bit frightened, remembering the war with Finland, which hadn't been at all awful, at least not for me nor for Leningrad. I sent my sister-in-law Olya and my nephew to the grocer's to buy something for dinner. Once I had fed my daughter, Shura and I went out into the street, me with the baby in my arms. Shura was soothing me, saying that the war wouldn't last long, although he and my husband would have to go and fight.

The point should be made that Lidiya Okhapkina's notes differ from Yura's and Kniazev's: they are not in the form of a diary, but are notes written slightly after the event, as Lidiya describes:

I started them on Victory Day itself. Everyone was celebrating, but I was overcome by a wave of feeling and I sat down to write. In particular, I was writing for my husband and for my son — my husband had fought outside the 'ring of steel' and my son had no memory of what had happened. And I vowed that I would write only the truth, and nothing but the truth! I wrote everything down within a month. At the time of the siege, I had no time to do it, absolutely no time at all, none whatsoever!

Her notes continue:

My husband got back on 26 June 1941. They had started to send some factory machinery out of Leningrad and also to evacuate some people. It was already difficult to obtain a railway ticket. All children of nursery-school age and all schoolchildren were supposed to be sent off to other cities, since Leningrad was going to be put in danger. My husband and I decided to send just our son, when his kindergarten went. My daughter and I would stay, and it

11

would make it easier for me to run to the bomb shelter if there were an alert. My husband was also predicting that the war would not outlast the summer, but would be over by winter!

On 28 June we sent our son off. Poor little fellow, he was only five years old! I had got his clothes ready for him and had marked every item, stitching his first and last names in thread. While I was dressing him that morning, I was wondering when I would next have to dress him. And I was abruptly overwhelmed by alarm and anxiety as to when I might ever see him again – what if he were lost all of a sudden? I got extremely distressed and agitated and, while I was telling my husband about it, I glanced at him and saw that there were tears running down his cheeks.

My husband left on 30 June. When he was leaving, he said that he was being sent to do a special job (he was an engineer), but not to the Front where the fighting was going on – for me not to be upset. This was both true and untrue. They sent him to somewhere near Smolensk and he found himself encircled by the Germans. He was wandering about and hiding in the woods for a long time, but just the same he got out in the end. However, neither he nor I knew this at the time.

The air raids usually went on for twenty or thirty minutes, but sometimes they lasted for an hour or two. I was all of a tremble with fear and white as a sheet. There was some kind of ringing in my ears and it seemed as though something had burst. My legs would give way and sometimes I was in no state to move. But I had to take my little daughter in my arms and run to the bomb shelter.

2

I Will Never Leave My City

Returning to Kniazev's diary:

1 July 1941. The 10th day of the war. Handing me a manuscript that he had been keeping at his house, Academician Pavlovsky said to me: 'Keep this safe, if at all possible. The situation is extremely grave.'

A bit later on, Gorodetsky, the Director of the Archives at the Institute of Russian Literature, came to see me. We discussed at length the issue of the safekeeping here in Leningrad of precious materials – the manuscripts of Pushkin, Lomonosov, Lermontov, Turgenev, Dostoievsky, Tolstoy and others. Gorodetsky looked dead on his feet. He is unable to sleep. 'What a heavy burden of responsibility you and I have to bear!' he said.

Indeed, we do bear the heaviest of responsibilities (and I am not speaking now of legal, administrative or official responsibilities) – the moral responsibility towards future generations.

2 July 1941. The 11th day. The Archive administration building on the Red Fleet embankment that has seen so much in its time is now living through one more phase in its history. By the staircase that once echoed to the clatter of the sabre worn by Officer of the Guard Lermontov, where, on the night of 15 December 1825, soldiers with fat candles stuck on the end of their bayonets came running pell-mell to search the building after the unsuccessful uprising in Senate Square – to the right there now hangs a short section of a girder on a thick wire and, beside it, a metal rod to

13

strike it with. This is for use in the event of a chemical attack. It is dark on the upper landing: it is lit only by blue-tinted light bulbs. I walked along the corridor in almost complete darkness and felt as though I were caught up in one of Meyerhold's stage sets.

The Archive storeroom at the Institute of Russian Literature produced a painful impression on me. The work rooms were unrecognizable. Everything was in a state of chaos. In the first anteroom, behind the statue of Alexander Veselovsky, two forty-pail barrels of water were standing, one of which was already leaking; everywhere there were shovels and boxes of sand; a fire-hose was stretched out along the corridor. Near the Pushkin Room were boxes for archive materials. Some of them were empty, others full. To give credit where it is due – the packing of the Pushkin materials couldn't have been bettered. But there was a great deal of nervous tension, confusion. Right beside the boxes, one of the archivists was dictating an article on fascism to a typist. Someone else was compiling a list of what was to be packed in the boxes. There was sand underfoot, puddles of water from the fire-hose snaking along the floor, apparently left there to dry out or else laid out there as some kind of safety requirement. People were jostling about everywhere, in the working areas of the Archives as well as on the Museum staircases, carrying sandbags. Two busts of famous writers were leaning beside the Reading Room doors. They had been removed from somewhere in a hurry and abandoned on the floor. Director Gorodetsky had done a great deal towards safe-guarding the materials, but he had perhaps got a bit ahead of himself. Uspenskaya, the daughter of the writer Uspensky and herself working in the Literature Archives, said to me, pointing to the mess: 'Perhaps we have actually overdone it...'

Gorodetsky himself was weary to the point of exhaustion. He had had no sleep for three or four nights in a row: he spends all his time at the Archives, stirring things up, constantly in conflict with the administration. Consequently, his nerves are totally shattered. 'I will definitely leave as soon as I have fulfilled my duty,' he told me. 'There is no question of me staying in charge of the Archives. They don't understand me, and the administrators reproach me for my obsessive preoccupation with the archived materials, for my perseverance...'

The monument to Peter the Great is being covered with sandbags.

In the little Rumiantsev Garden the trenches or dugouts have been completed.

The Sphinxes are still there. As always, they are sublimely indifferent!

I simply cannot make out whether what I hear is a noise inside my ears or the drone of propellers. It is now silent, menacingly silent. But you know that the moment will come when such silence will be shattered by a dreadful crash. Fires will break out. Huge buildings will be reduced to rubble under the impact of high-explosive bombs. People will be wounded, killed, driven crazy, flayed alive by shrapnel. All this will have to be endured, and endured probably in the very near future. If you allowed yourself to dwell on it all the time, you would undoubtedly go out of your mind or, at best, you would cease to be a viable human being and be reduced to an empty shell. I hope this won't happen to me. I still have plenty of zest for life.

3 July 1941. The 12th day. Those who heard Stalin himself speaking are saying that his speech was very hard to hear and that there were many parts of the speech that they found incomprehensible. My driver, who heard the speech, commented that Stalin's accent was extremely pronounced and that there were pauses during which you could hear the gurgle of water being poured into a glass.

It is going to be a fight to the death. In retreat, nothing must be left for the enemy. That was the gist of Stalin's speech.

5 July 1941. The 14th day. The whole morning my wife was clearing out the attic, carrying planks and all sorts of rubbish down to the courtyard. There was no end to the stuff that was thrown out of the attics, rubbish accumulated over more than a century. (Our building was radically restored six years prior to the first Patriotic

15

War, that is to say in 1806.) It is quite beyond our capabilities to organize an adequate and effective fire-watching rota for our staircase.

What sort of things am I, an avowed humanist, dreaming about nowadays? Here is an example, taken from a newspaper cutting: 'In response to the threat of a German invasion, the people of London have erected a scaffold near one of the buildings demolished during the Blitz, with the inscription: *Ready for Hitler.*'

However, he should not be hanged immediately, but brought to judgement first. Representatives of each of the countries destroyed by Hitler should be summoned: a man and a woman from particularly devastated areas should be invited to serve as members of the jury. Documents and examples taken from the countless mass of material evidence testifying to the monstrous cruelty of Hitler and the Nazis should be gathered together. A museum housing these 'relics' should be set up for the edification of posterity, to demonstrate to future generations the horrors and the suffering inflicted on people by the ruthless conqueror. Hitler's predecessors should find a place in this museum too – the world's killers and vandals, whether they met with good fortune or bad – such as Napoleon and Kaiser Wilhelm, Tamberlane and Attila, and other assorted scum of the so-called history of humanity or, to be more precise, of the history of pre-human society. Perhaps the place for Hitler is not even among this assemblage of the 'great', but simply in the ranks of stinking scoundrels like Cain, Herod and Judas. Names that are held in contempt the whole world over. Names that stink.

7 July 1941. The 16th day. A tense day. The air-raid siren sounded four times. We heard no shooting. They say that some lone enemy planes appeared over the city yesterday, but no alert was declared. Everyone says that an enemy plane was shot down over the outskirts of Leningrad and that, having crashed, it burst into flames.

St Isaac's, with its huge gilded dome visible many tens of kilometres away, like a lighthouse a hundred metres high, is losing its eye-catching appearance. The main gilded dome and the other small gilded domes are being smothered under some grey substance.

The Bronze Horseman has not yet been covered with sandbags; nor have the Sphinxes been covered at all. But Rastrelli's statue of Peter the Great, which used to stand in front of the Engineers' Castle, with the inscription: 'To Great-grandfather from his Great-grandson', has been dismantled. Only the bare pedestal remains.

Three days ago they were evacuating children. Now they are supposed to be evacuating not just children but adults too, if they are in a position to be able to accompany their children.

All the principal treasures of the Hermitage have been evacuated to parts unknown. Today Academician S.I. Vavilov came to see me. We decided to add our archive treasures as well to the second of the Hermitage special trains. Some we have already handed over to them: the mosaic portraits of Peter created by Lomonosov, two eighteenth-century maps of Petersburg (by Leblon and Makhayev) and the gilded casket kept in the Academy of Sciences in which reposes an Order of Catherine the Second's, written in her own hand.

There are no words to describe my state of mind when the mosaic portrait of Peter the First, founder of the Academy of Sciences, which I had been watching over with such love and care, was being taken down from the wall; when they were taking away the gilded casket, the *chef d'oeuvre* of a master craftsman of the eighteenth century; when the storehouse to which I had devoted so much energy and love was being stripped and pillaged. The Hermitage workmen carefully removed the portrait from the wall and carried it out to the waiting lorry. I saw them off – I can't conceal it – in great anguish. I was acutely aware that I might never see them again. To the best of my ability I had been building up the archives and museum of history of one sector of our great Russian culture – that of the Academy of Sciences. The war has disrupted the system and laid bare the places where these relics were kept with such loving care.

In the first instance we had considered keeping them safe *in situ*, but now, taking into account events at the Front, we are concerning ourselves with their evacuation; I think that evacuating them along with the Hermitage collection will be a safer thing to do... But my heart is aching. I went home feeling utterly desolate.

13 July 1941. The 22nd day. The car I was expecting never came and so for four hours I stood or sat under the columns of our academicians' home. Within the span of a few hundred metres (less than a kilometre) were spread before me the Neva, the bridge, the Sphinxes, the Academy of Arts, St Isaac's, the Admiralty spire, the monument to Peter (now hidden inside a casing of wooden planks), the former Senate building, the old houses along the embankment, the distant Winter Palace and, right by the bridge, the Rumiantsev House with its famous museum, and also the former English Embankment. Over to the west, the New Admiralty on the right bank of the Neva, the Baltic shipbuilding plant, the Institute of Mining, the Naval Academy, the former Kiev Church chapter house, the old straight streets of Vasilievsky Island, the ships standing at the jetties and the powerful tall cranes on the banks, where the Neva rounds the promontory of Vasilievsky Island. This is my city, whose beauty had once enraptured Dostoyevsky when he was standing on this very bridge, formerly the Nikolaievsky Bridge; here is the Senate Square and the vista opening up from it towards the Spit of Vasilievsky Island and the Academy of Sciences with the Pushkin House, whose praises were sung by the poet Blok; here is the proud monument to Peter the First, the Bronze Horseman, and here the Neva, celebrated by Pushkin; here are the Sphinxes which have given inspiration to many poets, artists and scientists who passed their way. A wonderful city! And can it really be true that it is threatened by the danger of an enemy occupation? No, no, no!

For four hours I was lost in admiration of the marvellous panorama of my native city. I will never leave it. If things turn out badly, it would be better to die here, somewhere along the embankment or in the deep waters of the Neva... But our city – and I firmly believe this – will never fall into the hands of the enemy!

15 July 1941. The 24th day. Today we transferred our greatest treasures from the Archives to the Hermitage: Lomonosov's and Kepler's manuscripts, the drawings from the Kunstkamera, and so on. They will be sent on the Hermitage's second special train to a place of safety. Which one? We don't know.

In all, thirty boxes were packed. We used everything we could to prevent the possibility of damp and dust penetrating them: tarpaper, cellophane, oilcloth, cardboard and wrapping paper. The Archive staff have worked solidly throughout the past two weeks. We compiled a list of contents for each box. The boxes were bound with wire and lead seals attached.

I accompanied the lorry with the boxes from the gateway out onto the embankment; the way you see off a loved one: a son, a daughter, a wife… For a long time I watched as the lorry made its way slowly across the Dvortsovy Bridge. (I had told the driver to go carefully.) I went back into the Archives feeling bereft.

Food ration cards are being introduced. The lists have to be drawn up by ten tomorrow morning. It is all being done in a big rush. The people themselves are fully in favour of this new or, to be more precise, this time-honoured initiative.

We have been ordered to hand over to our security department all Leningrad guides and street maps.

16-17 July 1941. The 25th and 26th days. Rumours are reaching us that there is a serious lack of coordination and poor organization. This scares me. What is it that is so frightening about the Germans? Precisely their exceptional organizational ability, their attention to detail, the smooth coordination of their actions…

The situation regarding the evacuated children is not good. Mothers are setting off to fetch their children. I gave our typist, T.K. Orbeli, permission to go to Borovichi to bring back her two daughters, aged nine and twelve.

3

The First Evacuation of the Children

In those days Maria Vasilievna Motkovskaya was directly involved in the evacuation of the children. She remembers the events in their full detail. By now no longer a young woman, she takes it hard to this very day that everything turned out the way it did:

'Nowadays, we understand that we were moving right into the path of the Germans, but no one realized that at the time. It seemed so straightforward. A very good region, a region deep in the country. And I was appointed as the person responsible to the District Executive Committee for getting the children out to the Novorodskaya region, specifically to Demiansk. And we went straight there. I had with me two passenger cars and a lorry. Two other comrades had been detailed to share the responsibility with me, and we set off.'

'And what was your job?'

'At that time I was Head of the Kirovsky District Department for People's Education – a member of the Executive Committee I was. That's why they sent me. I had a very good deputy, Anatoli Ivanovich Todorsky, who was responsible for sending the children, while my job was to make sure that they would be properly housed. And so I... I don't know if it's worthwhile telling you all this?'

'Please carry on.'

'This is how it happened. We arrived there... I must tell you that Demiansk had, as they say, got the whole region on its toes to receive the Leningrad children. We had worked out which school would be housed where, all that kind of thing. But a few days later the order came to evacuate the children again as a matter of urgency.'

'And you had actually brought the children there?'

'Yes, the children had been housed. But they only spent a couple of nights there, then came the order. And by then we were definitely getting the impression that the Germans were advancing fast.'

'And were there many children with you?'

'Many, very many.'

'Several hundred?'

'Not just hundreds – more than that! I can no longer tell you exactly how many. In round numbers, about 6,000 had been evacuated from the Kirovsky district, but some of them had later been sent on to the Yaroslavskaya region. So you see, it was a re-evacuation. Can you imagine what a saga it was? We also had nursery schools with us. We had brought out nursery-school children too, and they had to go back as well, almost without any rest. And the Germans were approaching hard and fast, you know. Demiansk is forty kilometres from Lychkovo railway station. The Germans had landed an exceptionally large airborne force there, and we found ourselves cut off. Later on they got our shock troops organized there and the whole of the landing force was scattered. So at that point we began to re-evacuate the children.'

'What were you using as transport for the return journey?'

'Oh! Anything we could lay our hands on! The army helped us enormously with this. Army vehicles began to take the children out. I can even remember a particular little incident: there I was, driving along, and I saw a bus parked by the side of the road – one with our children in it, that is. I jumped out. Why on earth had they stopped? They had to be got out as quickly as possible, you know! I approached: the driver was lying on the ground, asleep. I went up to him and called out: "Comrade!" And he said: "Well, now I can drive on. I've had no sleep for four nights, you see. I've had a bit of a rest and now I'll go on. The state I was in, I was afraid to drive any further." I remember it was a lovely day, a really beautiful day.

21

Then the bombing started in Lychkovo, at the railway station. At that time the children from the Dzerzhinsky district were in Lychkovo. They had gone even further than ours had. But where were the children? I dashed into some big building, because I knew that the children were always housed in good buildings. A teacher was sitting there. Surrounded by children. So many of them! And whenever a bomb exploded, they would cry out: "Mama! Mama! Mama!" Terrible! For the first time in my life, I told children a lie: "Don't be afraid! Don't be afraid! Those are ours!"

'I went out onto the porch myself. You know, he was flying so low, he would look, press – and a bomb would explode at once. They said afterwards that they hadn't known. Rubbish! They knew perfectly well and they could certainly see perfectly well. The fact of the matter was that the Dzerzhinsky district children were already boarding a special train at the time, and he was bombing the children in the station. Flawless weather. Children dressed in their best. He could see perfectly well who he was bombing… Well, later on, when we had got them all out of Lychkovo, I said that I would go back to Demiansk just the same, because I had to make sure that we had got everyone out.

'We got there. We rang round all the village councils: only the wounded ones had been left behind. And then – I remember it as though it were today – Vasili Yakovlevich and I were walking to the hospital where our children were; we were walking along and then there were some German prisoners being marched away. Apparently, several groups of paratroopers had landed there.

'I shouted out: "Damn you to hell! Just you wait! Just you wait! The time will come when our pilots will be killing your children too!"

'Vasili Yakovlevich said to me: "How could you say that, Maria Vasilievna? Can you imagine that our pilots would ever kill children? It is only they who kill like that."

'We began to move the wounded children out. We sent them off to Leningrad in good hands, with doctors and nurses. And we ourselves went on to the Kirovskaya region. Leningrad had sent my deputy there to help me. He had come to help because there was a really frightful to-do with the relatives and parents going on there! And who could blame them? For what could be more precious than a child?

'We hadn't got as far as Kotelnich station when the station-master came onto the train. He said: "Is the representative of the Kirovsky Executive Committee here?"

'I said: "Yes."

"You should know that there's been a message from the Kirov people advising you not to get off the train at Kotelnich."

'I said: "Why not?"

"There's a mob of parents waiting for you there!"

'You understand what had happened? The parents had arrived at Kotelnich, following along behind us. Do you understand?

'Anatoli Ivanovich, my assistant, said: "Maria Vasilievna, don't get out! Let me go instead!"

"Why should you? My conscience is clear. I will go myself. Don't even speak to me about it!"

'Well, we arrived in Kotelnich. I remember I had on such a pale coat, you know. I stepped down and an angry noise began to rise from the women. Well, they could see that I was composed.

'I said: "Comrades, let me tell you that if you behave like this, we will get nowhere. Ask me about whoever it is that you are worried about and I will answer every question, because all the children have been got out, except for those who had been injured."

"Those ones we met up with, those ones we saw" – this is what they were saying.

'I said to the parents: "I will say this to you before anything else: we got literally all of them out. There is only one little girl, Belova, that I am unable to tell you about..." Afterwards they began to question me about individual children. But I was unable to say where this one little girl was. Can you imagine? We checked the lists, rummaged through everything – nothing! I said: "Just you wait, I'll find her somehow!"

'And I remember this: I was wearing my pale coat. There were some railway sleepers there. I sat right down on them in that pale coat! And the women called out: "Stand up, stand up! What are you thinking of, sitting there? You will get that coat of yours dirty!" I could tell, you see, that the atmosphere had changed by then. Well, so much the better. For two days I stayed there in Kotelnich, hunting for that little girl all the time. She turned out to be in that very boarding school, but under a different surname.

'I said to her mother: "Get over there, that's where your daughter is." Then I went on to Kirov, and we settled down there.'

'Tell me, what happened to those children? Were they taken somewhere further east?'

'No, why should they be? The majority stayed in the Kirovskaya region, but that was not just our own evacuation zone, there were about 60,000 evacuated children there.'

But, come what may, many soon returned to Leningrad. Amongst those who did so were Alexandra Mikhailovna Arsenyeva and her daughter:

'When we were back in Leningrad, people would ask us: "Where have you come from, you refugees?" This in spite of the fact that I was born and bred in Leningrad, even my grandfather was a native Leningrader.

"You refugees, where have you come from?"

'And it was only the cashier in our local shop who recognized us and said: "Oh! These are actually neighbours of ours, they are from this very apartment building, I know them well!" '

'Did you come back looking so different from your previous selves, then?'

'When we got out of the railway carriage, some of us were in overcoats, some in dressing-gowns. We had been travelling towards Mga for a very long time, something like three days and nights. When the bombing began all down the carriages, there were dead and wounded straight away. We put the children under the seats, piled the mattresses on top of them, covered them with the mattresses, then threw ourselves on them.'

'Inside the carriages?'

'Inside the carriages. A bomb hit the steam-engine... In spite of that, when there was a bit of a lull, we managed to get out of the

24

carriage. By then it was starting to get dark. The station was on fire. There was no one to be found. It was a nightmare! The official in charge of the evacuation was sitting on a tree-stump and holding his head like this – clasping it in his arms. He had lost track of his family and he didn't know who was where. All it took was an outburst of firing somewhere – any kind of noise – we were straight into the ditch there and then, the children with their noses pressed into the dirt, and us on top of them. And we threw blankets over them. Afterwards, when we stood up, the children kept pulling them over their heads just the same. They covered themselves with those blankets like that. Well then, later on, we could make out something moving – all covered in fir branches. Apparently it was a camouflaged train. We made for the station, along the rails, we looked – a train! It was moving forward slowly, so slowly. It would stop and then move on again. It was all closed up. A soldier was standing in one of the doorways and he said: "Miss! Give me that mattress. I have a carriage full of wounded here." I gave him the mattress and I threw my daughter after it.'

'Where? Into the carriage?'

'Yes! I threw my daughter in and I said: "Take her!" And I intended to get in myself. But the wheels had started to turn. And my daughter was by then inside the carriage! Suddenly I saw that the wheels had stopped turning! I ran flat out. I caught up. I said: "Take me with you!" He said: "I can't! I can't! There isn't room to swing a cat! There's no place to strike a match. The wounded are groaning." I said: "Listen! I have a bottle of wine for the wounded. And I have something else in my rucksack." (I was carrying a big rucksack.) He said: "Well, get in here then!" I hurled the rucksack and jumped myself. He grabbed me by the back – I don't know how – and dragged me into the carriage. Afterwards I donated everything out of my bag to the wounded. My raisins, too, were handed round, and the wine was handed round. Everyone was groaning. I took my coat off, because they were freezing cold, the wounded. And when we had to unload the wounded at Sortirovochnaya, it turned out that my coat was all bloody. And I was left in just my dress, and it was hellish cold!'

'This was in September?'

'It was the thirtieth of September. They had already taken Mga. We arrived. They began to unload the wounded. They said to me then: "Your daughter is already in the station. You will find her there." And afterwards I found her. She was in the station, sitting at the foot of a column. Someone had given her a quilted jacket, she was huddled under the quilted jacket.'

'What is your daughter's name?'

'My daughter is Yevgenia Porfirievna Stroganova. She is a team leader in a design firm.'

'She was five years old at the time?'

'Yes, five years old. So my daughter actually saved my life. Or which of us saved the other – I don't really know. That's how it was. She's clever, not a chatterbox. After Mga she didn't speak for a long time, not to anyone. And when she went to school, she got "A"s, but she didn't speak…'

The children had to be retrieved from the areas where they appeared to be in danger as a matter of urgency. The Leningrad city organizations, together with the local authorities, were busy with this, as were some of the mothers themselves. Lidiya Okhapkina was attempting to bring back her son too:

One day after the shelling had stopped, I ran to get some bread with my little daughter in my arms – you had to take advantage of a lull. Ahead of me in the queue stood a woman of around sixty to sixty-three, wearing glasses, a cultured-looking lady, and she started to tell me that, once she had got her bread for two days in advance, she was going to fetch her grandson back. I asked her where her grandson had been sent. She answered that he had been evacuated with Kindergarten No. 21 – I remember the number exactly – that is, the same place where we too had sent our little son. Tentatively at first, I began to ask her if she would bring my boy back as well. She started to refuse, warning me that the roads were under bombardment and that, God forbid, they might be killed and she had no wish to burden her soul with a sin. Of course, I agreed with her, but I had no one else to turn to, and I clutched at her, if only in my mind, and began to beg and implore her so much that, in my distress, I even burst into tears. Then I took her hands and began to kiss them. And I kept repeating: 'Please, I beg you, have pity on him and on this little child in my arms. How could I travel with her? How would I be able to feed her? I beg you, please understand, help me, I will never forget you!' And other such words.

She agreed and even shed a tear herself. She asked me how old the boy was. I said that he would soon be six – I was lying – that he was sturdy, could run well and could walk a long distance, if he had to.

The following day I had to obtain the appropriate document for the return of the child from the District Council. I thought that this would be simple, but it turned out to be fairly complicated. When I got back to the Moskovsky District Council again, carrying my little daughter in my arms needless to say, a crowd of mothers had already gathered there. They were all upset, noisy, and some of them were even shouting: 'Bring our children back! It would be better if they were here with us, and if we have to die, then it will be together – at least we'll know how and where.' The man who was issuing the documents calmed people down as best he could, explaining that they had meant it all for the best and handing out the documents hastily. He gave me the power of attorney that I had asked for in favour of the woman. I went to her immediately. I gave her all the bread I had with me, and a little money. She left the very same day. And I began to wait impatiently for their return.

On one occasion I had only just returned from the bomb shelter after the all-clear had sounded, exhausted and weary. I lay down straight away and fell asleep. I was jolted awake by a terrible outbreak of shelling. Not having undressed at the time I fell asleep, I leapt up in my dress and stockings. I grabbed Ninochka, my rucksack in which the basic necessities for the infant were kept at the ready, my papers and my money. I rushed out of the room into the corridor. The window panes in my place had already been shattered a long time back and, at that moment, the door flew off its hinges from an explosive blast and its shock wave. I rushed out onto the porch and caught sight of shells flying right along our street and so low – roughly the height of the electricity poles. I didn't know what to do. I was afraid to run to the bomb shelter while the shells were flying there, while they were bombing. I was so frightened that my arms and legs were trembling and growing weak and my daughter was beginning to slip out of my arms. I sat down in the porch. My knees were shaking. A neighbour came running up to me and took the infant. 'Whatever are you doing, sitting here? Calm down, let's go to the bomb shelter,' she said. 'See, they are falling and exploding just a bit further away, somewhere over by the carburettor factory.'

Suddenly we heard the most dreadful explosion, and black smoke appeared. That shell had fallen somewhere quite near, where the oil-storage tanks were. They had managed to empty out the petroleum, however, but the huge, empty tanks remained, about the same size as our building, and it was there that the shell had fallen. There was a smell of burning. Saturated with paraffin and petroleum, the ground had caught fire, clouds of smoke and flames were spreading further and further all the time. And we were afraid that the fire might reach our building. The buildings nearest to ours burned down. The sky was a blackish crimson with reddish-yellow flashes.

I went back indoors. One of the neighbours, an old chap, re-hung the door for me, and I started to cook some watery semolina for my little girl on the paraffin stove. I made up my mind that, as soon as little Tolya had been restored to me, I would move out to somewhere else without any delay.

Two weeks passed. All that time Lidiya Georgievna lived under the dreadful strain of waiting for her son:

At last, I looked out of the window one day and saw the woman standing there with two little boys. One of them, of course, I rec-ognized as my own. I ran out as fast as I could, hugged him, began to kiss him and thank the woman. She started to describe what an extremely difficult journey it had been. They had ridden in a train for a while, and whenever it was bombed they would run out of the carriage. They had walked a great deal, had hitch-hiked rides on passing lorries, on horse-drawn carts... I thanked her. The next day I went to the District Council again to obtain travel permits. I had no idea where I was going to go. And it didn't matter to me – just as long as I got out of Leningrad. I would have liked to go to Saratov, where my mother was living, but it would have meant going through Moscow, and there were no trains going there. It was by then late August. But my trip never happened, because I lost little Tolya again.

When I arrived at the District Council, there were very many people outside its doors – mostly women, but there were some men as well. They all wanted to leave and had also come for travel documents. The front door was locked. Everyone was upset, shouting, banging on the door. I took Tolya off to one side, so that he wouldn't be crushed to death. Suddenly an air-raid warning sounded. They opened the door. I was shoved inside by the people behind me. I just had time to shout: 'Tolya! Run over here quickly!' – but then I looked around and couldn't find him. I asked them to open the door, but they wouldn't. I tried to get the documents as quickly as possible, asking to jump the queue, explaining that I had a child left out in the street. I was dreadfully agitated. When the all-clear sounded, I ran quickly out into the street, began to look for him, shouting: 'Tolya! Tolya!' – but he was nowhere to be seen. I started asking every passer-by: 'Have you seen a small boy, wearing a little white Panama hat and a blue coat, brown-eyed, five years old?' They all answered: 'No, no.' I would hurtle first in one direction then another, constantly repeating my question: 'Have you seen a little boy?' They all answered that they had not. Oh God, where is he now? What can I do? Where should I run? In such chaos, far from our home, he is bound to get lost. He seemed to know our address, but he might easily have forgotten it, got confused!

There were tanks driving along International Prospect and soldiers marching in formation. Many of them were wearing military uniform, but many others were in civilian clothes. They

29

were moving up to the Front. Those who were seeing them off — mostly women, of course — were walking behind or, rather, alongside the column. Some of them were crying. Ahead of them went a brass band.

The idea came to me that perhaps my son might have run along behind them. I raced after them, shouting all the while: 'Tolya! Tolya!' My daughter was sobbing in my arms. She probably needed feeding and was soaking wet. Having caught up with the column, I walked along beside it, looking all around and continuing to call out: 'Tolya! Tolya!' There were some people and soldiers who thought that I was calling out to one of them. Several turned to look. I was exhausted, my hair was in a mess. The beret I had been wearing had got lost. I could see that my son was not there, and I sat down in some doorway and started to cry. I thought: 'Well, that's the end of it. It means that I won't be leaving tomorrow; it means that I am doomed to remain in Leningrad.' A woman came up to me and asked me why I was crying. I explained to her that I had lost my little boy, and I was supposed to be leaving in the morning. She advised me to contact the militia, who should be able to help. When I got there and started to speak, the militiaman couldn't understand a thing, because I was speaking through choking sobs. He gave me a glass of water, to calm me down. When I had finally calmed down and explained the situation, the militiaman began ringing round the other militia posts, repeating that a little boy was lost, name of Tolya, who was to be brought to such and such a post. I waited for him until nine in the evening. My daughter was sobbing, I simply couldn't quieten her down. They suggested that I should go home, because it was not permitted to move around after nine o'clock without a special pass. I rode home.

All night long, it goes without saying, I was unable to sleep. Naturally, I was no longer giving any thought to my departure. Next morning I rode to the militia post. I saw little Tolya straight away. He was sitting on a windowsill, his cheeks smudged with tears. We were both overjoyed. He burst into tears. The militiaman said that he had kept on trying to board a tram, to get home, saying that his mother was waiting for him. He had taken a tram, ridden somewhere, but he hadn't known where to get off. He had certainly taken the wrong tram. Then he had started to cry. Some woman had taken him to the militiaman on duty and the latter, as soon as he had been relieved, had taken him to a militia post, but a different one, where he had spent the night. And it was only in the morning that he had been brought to this post.

It was half-past ten in the morning, and we had been due to leave at eight. We were already too late. I didn't feel up to applying for the documents again that day or the next. This business of losing my son was the deciding factor in my not getting out of Leningrad.

4

The Small World of Georgi Alexeievich Kniazev

19 July 1941. The 28th day. While I was sitting in the garden during the alert, my faithful companions – the Sphinxes – seen from an unfamiliar angle, were silhouetted against the background of the bright July sky. The sunlight was reflected from their glossy chestnut backs. So many of my thoughts and images are associated with them, relating both to the past and to the future. I am here only fleetingly, they are virtually eternal. Even if a high-explosive bomb were to fall near them, it is unlikely that both the Sphinxes would be destroyed; one of them would most probably remain. And my writings and my verses have been so closely linked with the Neva Sphinxes for many years, with my thoughts, my anxiety, with a 'premonition' or 'forecast' of what was to come. Naturally, I was not able to imagine all the events specifically, but I did foresee the dark night of the great humanistic tradition. Up ahead, in the distance, there will be dawn again, sunshine once more. But here and now is the terrible black and bloody night of civilization. Your heart bleeds when you think that what the Soviet people have constructed since the October Revolution, with such toil and heroism, is being totally annihilated. A terrible hatred grips you when you think about the conquerors, with their daydreams of bending all the conquered to their will, like slaves. But we will not be the conquerors' slaves! We have a sacred aim – to defend ourselves against the vandals. For what do the conquerors bring to the world?

Domination by the 'élite' castes, the rulers, the builders of the New Order...

I was sitting in the garden and this prospect was clouding my mind. I looked at the Sphinxes: 'You have seen it all, but you have not yet had occasion to see human misfortune on such a dreadful scale. The whole world is in flames! And the frightful muzzles of the ruling jackals with their superb technology nose through the ashes of the old world! You, my Sphinxes, were created in slave-ridden Egypt. But that was 3,500 years ago. Is it possible that you will once more stand silently amidst a once free people, turned into slaves?'

How welcome it was to hear the harmonious notes of the all-clear. Everyone emerged from the dugouts and went about their business or continued along their way...

20 July 1941. The 29th day. There is a need for organization, for really stringent discipline. And that is in short supply with us! We have not yet been capable of working in an organized and coordinated way. Only under wartime conditions are we learning. Wherever I am at all able to do so, I try to inculcate a mood of cheerfulness and determination. But I am truly just a grain of sand in an immense sea of people.

The desk lamp is shaded on three sides, so that the light falls only on the table and does not illuminate the corners of the room. I am writing these lines and thinking: 'Who knows, perhaps in a few days' or a few hours' time, nothing but ashes will remain of all these screeds of writing?' But I go on writing just the same. I am trying to convey the kind of thing that others will not record, even trivialities, even details like the wife of the academician Alexeiev sitting out her turn of duty at the gateway in a hat and kid gloves.

Today in the Rumiantsev Garden I saw that workmen and office workers had gathered at the little tables there to play dominoes. All exactly the same faces as were there three or five years ago. They go on playing as if nothing had happened. When there is an alert, they slide down into a slit trench. In the streets there are people passing by, trams rattling along, little boys dashing about. At the moment they are swarming, particularly over my favourites – the Sphinxes. They clamber over the back, over the head of a once proud ruler turned into stone, poking sticks into its eyes, into its ears. Beside the Sphinxes, piles of sand have been deposited. Women, girls and adolescent boys are shovelling it up. They are piling it into vehicles. The city is living a life of intensive labour. No irritability whatsoever, no depression can be detected. Only the flow of transport has sharply decreased. To make up for it, lone military vehicles fly past at an incredible speed and are not very heedful of the traffic regulations. When I am in my wheelchair I therefore prefer to travel on the pavement and at a speed not exceeding a normal walking pace.

I got into conversation with the manager of our building. 'It is regrettable,' he said, 'that they are fighting on our territory. There will be a great deal of destruction. Why did they give up the fortifications along the old borders of the State without a fight?' I was unable to give him an answer. We have very little information. I simply don't even know whether the Germans are near or far. Is Leningrad under serious threat or not?

On this lovely summer's day Leningrad is really full of people. There are many strollers on the embankment in the evening. There is peat smouldering near Leningrad, and a haze hangs over the city. It is simply incredible that we are at war: everything is so peaceful, at least outwardly. The area around the Sphinxes offers a whole range of recreation for both adults and children. In spite of the evening hour, there are little boys swimming there. Up until now, we have seen neither wounded nor refugees. Wherever has the stream of people from the Western Ukraine, Western Byelorussia, Lithuania and Latvia been directed?

I was watching a mother – our caretaker – with her child. Such a tranquil idyll, but she has her gas mask with her. She is playing with the child, but she is also keeping a close eye on the sky – might they be flying? And how many such mothers have lost their children, the roof over their heads, their lives?

I am becoming unbearably heavy-hearted. I am afraid of the poisonous fumes of chauvinism no less than of the Nazi contagion. For us the war is something holy, because we are defending ourselves against swooping vultures; it is not a war fought to establish the supremacy of one nation over another. The question now arises as to the extent of the guilt of the German people, bringing so much suffering to mankind. What would Hitler have done if he had not had the support of a significant sector of the German people? Agonizing question...

10 August 1941. The 50th day. How everything is changing. Only a year ago we were burying England as a naval and world power. Now England's ships are not just an open coffin, floating on the ocean waves. With the help of the USA, England is maintaining her dominion over the seas. And England is not an enemy, but an ally. Together with England we are fighting a common adversary – Hitler's Germany. And how outdated that image of a floating coffin seems now!

The political world has gone through so many unforeseen and unexpected twists and turns in recent years. As simple people, albeit historians, we find it hard to grasp all this. So I don't attempt to analyse it too much. I just state the facts. Last year we were not even able to imagine what is going on now. What will next year have in store for us? Communism is really just as alien to a liberal-conservative bourgeois democracy like England as it is to Nazi Germany... So many inconsistencies!

11 August 1941. The 51st day. Our boiler man Urmancheiev has left to join the army. He leaves behind three small children and a young, but not awfully bright wife. Just after he had left, having endured a painful scene of farewell, entrusting his wife and children to our care, we learned that the compulsory evacuation of children under fourteen and their mothers had been announced. The bombing of Leningrad is inevitable, and anyone who spreads the opinion that the Germans will not bomb Leningrad is either a dedicated *agent provocateur* or a chattering fool. Children and their mothers must get out of Leningrad by compulsory order. Two departure dates have been set: the fifteenth for non-working mothers, the twenty-third for those who have jobs. The evacuation will take place by barge. The mothers are in despair. Whatever will they do, however will they live in the places that they are evacuating them to?

For my collection of 'signs of progress': an illustration from the magazine *Ogoniok*, 11 June 1941. The memorial to the English poet Milton has been destroyed by the bombs of Hitler's gangsters. This was in England. What has been destroyed in the cities of the Western Ukraine, Western Byelorussia and Lithuania? So far we have no photographs. Clearly, it would be a very comprehensive collection.

14 August 1941. The 54th day. Today was an excruciatingly exacting day. Something bad has happened at the Front. At midday the news came that Smolensk had fallen. This news fell on my heart like a stone. The Germans are somewhere on the other side of Lake Ilmen. The city is full of every possible kind of rumour. The women are in a particularly nerve-racked state. Up until recently they were holding out. Now their nerves are giving way. What had so gladdened me – the calmness, the self-control – has come to an end. One woman, unwilling to plunge her child into all the ordeals, was told at the District Council: 'If you don't want to leave in an organized fashion, later you will be making your way on foot.' Whatever is this? Preparation for the evacuation of the whole population, for the surrender of Leningrad? Today even the stoical people have got cold feet.

At the moment I have been trying to read a history of mankind that I had started, but I was unable to overcome my fatigue. There was no opportunity to take a rest today: it turned out to be quite a day. I am gathering all my strength within myself, so as to surmount all obstacles. Fate is making me a witness or, more precisely, a contemporary of the most extreme and most stupendous events. Smolensk also fell in 1812. The Battle of Borodino was fought on the twenty-sixth of August. In September Napoleon entered Moscow. How will events unfurl this time? And where do the Germans get so much strength from, so much diabolical energy?

My wife said to me: 'I love life, I love Nature – I have done since childhood...' She is stoically and courageously living through these hard days. She is ready for anything, as I am too. A wonderful, remarkable woman! What if fate should separate us, force one of us to witness the collapse or death of the other? If we have to die, then let it be together...

So now the night is nearly over. It is getting light. My turn on watch is coming to an end. There were no alerts. The Germans have once more failed to bomb Leningrad. This gives rise to considerable amazement and to a host of rumours, sometimes primitive in the extreme. Up to and including one about Hitler's daughter requiring the magnificent northern capital to be left intact!

What will the day bring today? There are two hours left for sleep before setting off for the Archives. My heart feels as if someone had trodden on it; squashed it. It is bleeding. Perhaps that time is not far distant when...I will not think ahead at all. I will be good, energetic, hardworking. Until the end.

In front of me there are three portraits: Leo Tolstoy, Turgenev and Chekhov. And to one side – Dostoievsky. They taught me love for my fellow man, for mankind; they were great humanists. I shall remain true to my teachers!

In the newspapers there are many declarations, expressions of sympathy, etc., on the part of America, England, and other countries. I am fed up with reading paper offers of help... So far there is no sign of a Second Front against the Germans!

23 August 1941. The 63rd day. During the night of 22 August, and then again on the 23rd, we were expecting bombing raids on Leningrad. The 22nd marked two months of war and a month from the day of the first raid on Moscow. They chose this number by black magic. But there was no bombing at all. No one can understand the reason why the Germans are leaving Leningrad untouched. On this issue, all kinds of fabrications continue to spread.

We are all now living in the hope that, driven back towards the sea, the Germans will be taken prisoner or annihilated by the naval cannon of the Baltic Fleet. We have even calmed down a bit. We spent the whole day today in this hope: that the Germans would be driven away from Leningrad. We live in another hope too: that in the south Budyonny's army was able to escape from the noose!

25 August 1941. The 65th day. The information provided is utterly inadequate. With one accord it all indicates that the positions at Kingisepp are in our hands, Smolensk too... But the situation in the south is difficult. A colleague informed me in confidence today that the fate of Leningrad will be sealed any day now: the city will be declared indefensible. Which is why there are no air raids. Which is also why the evacuation of mothers and children has been suspended. An area with a radius of thirty kilometres will define the city limits. It is extremely difficult to get out of Leningrad at the moment... After his visit I began to feel wretched: is it really impossible for us to drive the Germans away from Leningrad? That's the whole point: how is it that suddenly and with such immediacy there is monstrous pressure on the south and the north-west, that is, on us? Where did the enemy find such overwhelming strength? I am looking events calmly in the face, but it saddens me that we are insufficiently well-organized to overcome all the hardships of war...

5

I Am Sixteen

Yura Riabinkin was busy all through those weeks of summer – going to the Pioneer Palace, playing chess, reading – what else would a Leningrad schoolboy be doing in that late wartime summer?

Went to the cinema with Dodya, saw *The Boxers*. Went to the zoo, played billiards, played chess... For some reason my chest has started to ache badly. I've developed a cough. Sweat simply pours off me day and night...

It seems highly likely that the city of Ostrov has been taken, since it lay in the path of the Pskov offensive. Which front is Voroshilov commanding? Mother has been ordered to report to the Baltic railway station to travel to Kingisepp to dig trenches. I accompanied her to the station.

When we got home in the evening, Tina had unexpectedly arrived from Schlüsselburg. She is to be appointed senior doctor at the hospital. We came to an agreement that, if anything should happen to Mother, she would take me and Ira in with her. There is talk that school will start up again this winter, but I don't particularly believe in it. You would have to be still alive here.

This war is likely to be the hardest and the most dangerous for us. The price of victory will be very high.

Mother gave me some money which I spent on a bowl of beetroot soup and a plate of buttered semolina in the canteen where she works. Then I went home. At home I studied how to reach checkmate using bishops and knights.

I read *David Copperfield*.

I went with Mother to where they are constructing the fortified lines at Tolmachevo, in the Luga area.

Yura describes enthusiastically how he dug anti-tank ditches alongside the adults. Those two weeks of August were filled with air-raid alerts; they were fired on by Messerschmitts, but they dug; dug for eight hours at a stretch. In the meantime Yura's pals were starting to leave Leningrad, and Yura's mother, too, was getting ready for evacuation. They discussed where they might go. Yura's mother wanted to be near Leningrad, but for some reason Yura favoured Omsk. He was following events at the Front with ever-increasing intensity, mulling them over and becoming dissatisfied with his own passive role.

26 and 27 August 1941. Novgorod was taken several days ago now. Leningrad is exposed to the danger of being cut off from the rest of the USSR. They are sending us a steady stream of American tanks and planes ('Boeings'). These Boeings are transported by ship as far as Vladivostok, and from there they fly on to Leningrad, making landings on the way. The Japanese recently made an official protest about the Americans sending petroleum to us, claiming that this threatened their interests. It wasn't done without support from Germany, that's for sure! Our forces have met up with the English in Iran... Iran is the world's fourth largest producer of petroleum.

I keep myself busy with things that are not really very useful. I read books, play chess, spend time on military matters, play war games.

No further news of Tina.

30 August 1941. Mother wants me to put my name down for the Naval Cadet School. But I know very well that the Medical Board would not pass me, so I am rejecting the idea. All the same it is hard to put aside one's dreams – of a life at sea – but there is nothing to be done about it. It would be pointless to keep on trying.

A whiff of pessimism.

I will spend the days on military matters, playing chess and reading. A terribly depressed mood. I can see no future prospects for myself, not even mediocre ones. Mother is going to let Nina go from the first of September. Chess, war games, military matters. What is there for me now, when my own secret dream in life – joining the Navy – has become unattainable? It is hard to bear. I feel utterly pessimistic.

31 August and 1 September 1941. Today, 1 September, there was no teaching at school. No one knows when there will be. From the first of September food products can be bought only with ration cards. Even matches and salt are being rationed. Famine is approaching. Slowly but surely.

Leningrad is surrounded! A German airborne force landing near Ivanovskaya railway station has cut our city off from the whole of the USSR.

Rotten mood. I don't know whether I will ever recover my cheerfulness.

Today, probably because of carrying heavy sacks at Mother's work place – I was helping to remove valuable papers – I strained my neck.

In the bulletins they write that fighting is continuing on all fronts. Just that. At night flashes light up the sky. Long-range guns are striking the enemy from our firing positions. The enemy is fifty kilometres from Leningrad!

I frittered the whole day away. (Excepting only that I helped with the work at Mother's place.) I talked to Finkelstein. If there is going to be no teaching in the schools, we are going to work through (if we can!) all the courses for class nine together. We have the necessary textbooks.

Tomorrow is my sixteenth birthday. I am sixteen!

2 September 1941. Well, there was nothing unusual to mark my birthday.

Mother gave me five roubles for the canteen. I decided to cheer myself up. I went shopping and bought a chess manual. Later on I called in at the canteen – there was nothing cheap there at all by then. To make up for it, Mother came home in the evening, bringing me two little pies. Afterwards we made a new lot of soup, and I even ate some of that. Full, contented!

6

Learning from the Stoics

On Yura Riabinkin's birthday, G.A. Kniazev was writing:

2 September 1941. The 73rd day. Leningrad has become a front-line city. The newspaper didn't come. On the display board by the University, the latest news bulletins had been posted. Brief, stereotyped communiqués: 'Battles are in progress along the entire Front.' 'Our troops are advancing in Iran.' There are always four, five or ten people standing by the display board. It's a pity I can't provide a picture of them.

In the newspapers and over the radio there are rallying-calls for the defence of Leningrad: 'Let us defend each street, every single square, make each building a fortress!' But somehow something has gone wrong with the People's Army again. And around me, in my own small circle, there are so far no barricades, no trenches, no People's Army detachments.

Yesterday, about twelve o'clock at night, there was the thunderous roar of the long-distance guns firing or the din of explosions. In the sky there was the flare of distant fire. The precise whereabouts of our own troops is unknown to us, but the reality is that Leningrad is surrounded by enemy troops. Today the bread ration was reduced, the commercial shops were shut down. We are entering into the position of a besieged city. We are facing the coming ordeal directly and calmly. Evidently, it has been decided to defend the city, and not to surrender. Those who govern us know best. They have to make the strategic decisions. In this titanic struggle Leningrad is no more than an episode... But we Leningraders are living people, and for us, unarmed civilians not fighters, decisive events are taking place. But for now I have once more switched on the lamp under its green lampshade and have settled down at my writing desk. And what is to come in a few days' time, no amount of imagination could possibly envisage. Only parallels with the crushing defeat and destruction of tens and hundreds of cities arise in the fragmentary information provided by the newspapers like bad dreams in the night. But no parallel is valid, when it is a question of such a colossus as Leningrad. Can it really be that I will witness her destruction?

The Sphinxes are visible from the garden over to the right. They are standing as they always have done. They have simply been forgotten about... They're not at the top of the list! And they too – they keep to themselves, above events.

After last night's disturbances, I removed from the walls of my office at work the academicians' portraits in silhouette by Anting (1783) in their glass frames, so that they would not fall and get broken. I placed flat on a ledge in the wardrobe a vase of the earliest Soviet porcelain, specially made for the 200th anniversary of the Academy of Sciences, so that it would not topple over when the building was shaking. I hadn't done this earlier, so as not to disrupt the orderliness which had been helping us to organize our willpower, our thinking... Events have occurred which we never thought we would live to see or bear witness to... Leningrad is under the threat of a deadly peril!

5 September 1941. The 76th day. We had begun to take our dinner in the academic canteen, but now there are long queues there.

The weather is cold and rainy. The flowers along my way to work have withered, wrinkled, they are living out their last days. The Sphinxes are gleaming, wet with rain. Above the Neva a grey haze masks the clean outlines of St Isaac's, the Admiralty, the Winter Palace, the Senate, and the stallions above the arch of the General Staff building. And somewhere, a few tens of kilometres away at the approaches to Leningrad, there are Germans... It is not to be believed, it is like a feverish dream, not a reality at all. How could this have happened? Germans at the gates of Leningrad!

The manager of our building, having taken a seat at the entrance, shared his impressions with me: 'If there had been the sort of organizing earlier on, that there is now, the Germans would never have been allowed to approach so near to Leningrad.'

7 September 1941. The 78th day. The Stoics taught that the aim of life was to acquire wisdom and virtue. The only way to achieve this was through mastery over one's passions and unwise inclinations, and a steadfast indifference towards the vicissitudes of fate. It is true that amongst the Greeks there were also followers of another school of philosophy, which held that the goal of life was happiness.

Life is teaching us a steadfast indifference to the vicissitudes of fate. And I am sometimes drawn towards such a philosophy. But I am not a philosopher, nor a thinker in the full sense of that word. I want to live well, happily. My personal dream – of happiness – is closer to that of those other Greek thinkers...

Today is Sunday. I don't know what is going on in the world, in the surroundings of my city, in Leningrad itself. I don't feed on malicious rumours, I maintain no correspondence; I sit and read isolated pages from histories of all times and peoples. And on each page alongside the genial thoughts and creativity of man, there is also his blood – bloodshed and inexpressible suffering.

I live only in the present minute, not even the hour; I don't speak about days any more. Fate has granted another minute – and I am grateful to her. I read, I write, I think... And what there will be even a minute later, I try not to think about.

A small picture caught my eye: 'Peaceful Old Age'. In the illustration there is a very old man reading in peace and tranquillity. How ironic to be appreciating this in the current hell!

There is another picture more appropriate to our times. The great geometrician Archimedes is sitting pondering over his drawings. And enemies have already burst not only into the city,

45

but even into the house where the great philosopher is living. They halt for an instant, catching sight of the old man's peaceful expression. A fine legend has it that, when he realized that it was his drawings, not himself, that were threatened with destruction, he said: 'Don't destroy my circles (the drawings).' It is well known that Archimedes was killed by the Romans during the siege of Syracuse in the year 212 BC.

7

The First Bombardment

Returning to Yura Riabinkin's diary:

5 and 6 September 1941. Mother is after me again to apply for admission to the Naval Cadet School, but I don't feel like giving it a try. It makes no odds because the school wouldn't accept me in any case. For one thing, I have poor eyesight, and for another I have pleuritic adhesions in my right lung, and probably something else wrong as well. What is the point of entertaining high hopes, only to reap bitter disappointments later on?

Leningrad is being shelled by long-range German guns. There is a constant din of exploding shells. Yesterday a shell fell on a building in Glasovskaya Street, demolishing half of it. Finkelstein and Nikitin had been to see it and they told me about it. Another shell fell in a public garden somewhere – there were many dead and wounded. Today there was shelling again towards the evening. There was a continual racket of shells falling over towards the Moscow railway station, then further away on the other side of it. In the queues the women are saying that Hitler has vowed to bring the war to an end by 7 September, which is tomorrow. That's quite a rumour! Mind you, only a very short while ago they were saying exactly the same thing, only the date then was 2 August.

Yesterday I called at Shtakelberg's. He wasn't at home. No sooner had I got back home than he turned up at my place. He is working at the hospital as a medical orderly and is responsible for admitting the wounded. He and I went together to an exhibition about the

Great War. There were many interesting things to see. There was a medium-sized French tank on display there and a light Czechoslovakian one, then a 142mm howitzer and all kinds of German shells and equipment. There were posters, photographs and other such exhibits mounted on the walls. We were caught by an air-raid alert and spent three hours at the exhibition. Shtakelberg told me about the Germans' chemical weapons. Terrifying things!

It is now half-past nine. Leningrad is under fire from the Germans' heavy long-range guns. Powerful explosions are making the buildings and windows shake.

7 September 1941. Mother has a day off work. I had to be on duty at the gates from twelve noon until four in the afternoon. I read *Burning Daylight* by Jack London.

Yesterday, the 6th, there was intensive artillery fire. The Germans were striking Leningrad with their heavy guns. Today it has been more calm. There was no alert sounded, but the anti-aircraft guns were in action. It is the 129th anniversary of the Battle of Borodino today. A most almighty battle between the Russian and the French armies took place at that time outside Moscow. More than 108,000 men were killed or wounded on that day. On that occasion the foreign invaders met with a fierce rebuff.

8 September 1941. A day of alerts, disruptions and ordeals. I will describe everything in order as it happened.

In the morning Mother came running home from work, saying that they were sending her to work on a collective farm, situated near Oranienbaum. She would have to leave me and Ira on our own. She had been to the District Council and had been granted a postponement until tomorrow. Later on we had a discussion about the Naval Cadet School. Mother went to the Regional Party Committee and from there called in at the Cadet School, while I went round to Finkelstein's place. They had had quite a lark at their school. The lads had been told to cover the attic floor with whitewash. However, the whitewash had turned out to be insuffi-

48

cient for the task, so they had decided to dilute it. But they had used superphosphate instead of whitewash and a chemical reaction had occurred, as a result of which chlorine gas was given off. The lads had been obliged to go around the attic with their gas masks on. Varfolomeyev had arrived and had lost his temper. ('My efforts to teach you chemistry appear to have been in vain!') Afterwards Dodya had gone to surrender his bicycle to the army. (A notification about the 'mobilization' of bicycles had arrived three days earlier.)

When I got back home, Mother was already there. She told me that there was a possibility that they might accept me. But I doubt that very much indeed. Then Mother went off somewhere else.

And that was when it started to get really terrible.

They sounded the alert. I didn't even pay any attention to it. But then I heard a noise break out in the courtyard. I looked out of the window. First I looked down below, then up above and I saw twelve Junkers. The sound of bombs exploding boomed out. Deafening explosions came one after the other, but the window panes didn't rattle. The bombs were evidently falling some way away, but they were extraordinarily high-powered ones. Ira and I hurtled downstairs. The explosions were coming non-stop. I started to run back towards our place. Zagoskin's wife was standing on our landing. She had got scared too and had dashed downstairs. I struck up a conversation with her. Then Mother came running in from somewhere, having forced her way through the streets. Soon afterwards they sounded the all-clear. The outcome of the Nazi bombing raid turned out to be utterly devastating. Half the sky was shrouded in smoke. They had bombed the harbour, the Kirov Plant, and that area of the city in general. Night fell. A sea of flames could be seen over towards the Kirov Plant. Little by little the fire subsided. Smoke; smoke penetrated everywhere and we could detect its acrid odour even here. It left a little sting in the throat.

Yes, it was the first real bombardment of the city of Leningrad.

Now night has fallen, the night of 8 to 9 September. What does this night have in store for us?

Around midnight. As soon as Ira had gone to bed, the air-raid warning sounded again. We went down to the ground floor. We had quickly put our clothes on. At first there was a little firing from the anti-aircraft batteries, then came the whine of aircraft and the crackle of their guns. Searchlights were probing the sky the whole time. But not a single plane was shot down. Somewhere was getting bombed again. All the residents of the lower two floors (excluding the basement) had gathered in the ground-floor corridor. For ages, time dragged heavily by. Then, somewhere in the courtyard of Building 36, we heard them banging on a metal girder. We were petrified. Maruska, Lidka and I put on our gas masks and went out into the courtyard to ask what it meant. And the man on duty in the courtyard replied that there had been no alert whatsoever for a chemical weapon attack. Nearly two hours passed like this. Finally we decided to go back home. The alert was still in force. The glow to the east had died away, but time and again German planes flew past over the city at lightning speed. They were being shot at, but they kept on and on flying over the city in waves. Right now I don't know what to do. Mother and Ira have gone to bed without undressing. Perhaps I should do the same. I can't make up my mind. Yes, this is a week that the Nazis intend us to have fixed in our minds, in the minds of all Leningraders. Obviously, they did not succeed in taking Leningrad on the ground, so now they have decided to destroy her from the air.

9 September 1941. I am writing this at midnight precisely. During the course of the past day there were eleven alerts! And what alerts they were! Lasting for an hour, for two. The most terrible alert was the most recent one, tonight. They bombed heavily in the Octyabrsky district. Bombs also exploded in Krasnaya Street and in Theatre Square, also by the Lieutenant Schmidt Bridge. An eyewitness arrived from there all covered in mud – he had been splattered with dirt – and he told us all about it.

During one of the daytime alerts they shot down a solitary aeroplane above our building. The pilot, wearing a parachute, jumped out directly into the city. I don't know what became of him. It's more than likely they caught him. I didn't go to the Cadet School, I didn't go to ordinary school. The intervals between alerts lasted about ten to fifteen minutes. Tomorrow, all being well, Mother has ordered me to go to the Cadet School. I don't imagine that the doctors will pass me as fit. I will not get through the medical exam.

In the news bulletin they broadcast that an air attack on Leningrad had taken place at half-past eight, but that no military targets had been harmed. However, Mother said that many food-storage warehouses were on fire, also the Vitebsky goods yard, the creamery and several apartment buildings as well – no one knows how many.

Everyone puts these air raids on Leningrad down to the fact that Hitler's operation to seize the city with ground forces did not succeed. Embittered by this, he ordered the bombing.

On the various fronts nothing has changed. We recaptured some town by the name of Yelnya.

There will be no respite for Leningrad now. They will come here every day to bomb.

They want to allot a room in our apartment to the family of some sort of chief engineer to a group of companies. Bastards! Mother intends to refuse point-blank.

The siren. One o'clock. An alert. The all-clear. Interval between the two: ten minutes. Another alert. That's how to reduce the whole population to total exhaustion. And at our own building there is not even a bomb shelter.

Perhaps I will get myself fixed up with the fire-watching brigade at school. There's no way I am going to make it to the Cadet School. I shall go to bed while it's quiet. After that, who knows?

That same day of the first bombardment was experienced differently by G.A. Kniazev:

8 September 1941. The 79th day. When I was returning from work, in a sector of my small world – the Neva embankment – I sensed an erratic beat in the life of the city. The Nikolaievsky

51

Bridge was open. The only movement of traffic taking place was across the Dvortsovy Bridge alone. So the normally deserted University Embankment had been turned into a main thoroughfare. Soon, between the raised arms of that beauty of a bridge, a ship appeared — a warship with two long-range guns. The ship was heading upstream along the Neva. The river was busy. Naval motor launches were stirring up the leaden September waters of the Neva. Not far from the Dvortsovy Bridge the ship came to a standstill and gave a prolonged whistle, so that further on they would make way for her more quickly.

Along the embankment came a detachment of sailors in field uniform and with steel helmets on their kitbags. Some kind of motor vehicle, all covered in mud, its glass shattered, drove past. In the little Rumiantsev Garden, groups of Leningraders were again waiting to be sent off on their work assignments. Armed and unarmed workers were being taken somewhere in buses...

So, like a river at high tide, my deserted path along the rows of flowers and shrubs was suddenly filled with life...

Incidentally, they were trimmed the other day. Even in these terrible times, someone was watching over them! Somehow this strengthened me, buoyed me up.

In Siezdovskaya Street people were swarming round the barrack gates. They were waiting to see the wounded billeted there. Some were peeping in the windows, where Red Army soldiers and sailors with bandaged heads or arms were leaning out...

At half-past seven in the evening, when I was having a rest, the whole of our building suddenly began to shake. There was an outburst of firing from the anti-aircraft guns and the machine-gun batteries. The first moment was frightful. But at once I pulled myself together, resisting the first impulse to get out, to run from danger... In the courtyard, people were crowding around the bomb shelter... Everyone was gazing up at the sky. Some neighbours came to say that from their windows a colossal glow to the south could be seen, and columns of black smoke that blotted out the whole sky. Indeed, when I went to take a look, there was a fire blazing the other side of the Neva. It was even reflected in the water. Some were speculating that, having broken through, German bombers had succeeded in setting fire to the oil reservoir somewhere near Volkhov Village.

Half-past ten. An alert again. I went out into the stairway. Searchlights were probing the sky. The anti-aircraft guns were firing. I came back inside to my study and I am sitting by the lampshade of my green desk lamp, wearing my overcoat, my cap and my galoshes, and I am writing... My wife jokes: 'You are just like Archimedes.' The building shudders, but not the way it did earlier. Before the alert, I managed to phone the office. Everyone on duty there was at the ready. My wife and I had our supper. We made up our little bundles with our things and money in. My wife left for her first-aid post.

Half-past midnight. The alert is still in force. There are occasional outbursts of firing from the ships in the Neva. The neighbours have still not returned; they are sitting on the steps downstairs. By the looks of things, the whole of Leningrad will go without sleep tonight.

Thus, on the seventy-ninth day, the bombing of Leningrad began. No doubt many more such troubled days and nights lie in store for us up ahead. We will have to drain the cup of tribulation to its dregs, a bitter cup.

10 September 1941. The 81st day. It turned out that yesterday too there were victims during the evening raid. The bastards were dropping bombs again – on the zoo. The elephant perished. According to one source of information, it received contusions from a bomb blast, but according to another, it was injured by shrapnel. It was in great pain, and they shot it. Two evenings running, the unfortunate zoo has suffered all the horrors of a real hell.

Among the burning buildings that added to the pall of smoke hanging over Leningrad on the night of the first bombardment was the fat-manufacturing plant where Nina Alexandrovna Abkina worked as an engineer. What follows is an extract from an interview with her:

'As soon as I had finished with the Institute and had qualified as a production engineer, I was posted to Leningrad. That was because the topic of my diploma dissertation had been the margarine industry and, at that time, they were building a margarine factory there. One had already been built in Moscow and a second was under construction in Leningrad. They sent me to that one.

'There had been a factory there in the past, during the time of the Tsars, mainly for the processing of Russia's home-grown linseed crop. The linseed fat was processed into linseed drying oil. They were already producing a great deal of it when I started working there – we were turning out 10,000 tons a year of this natural drying oil. We needed to broaden our raw material base and, with this in view, we began to take in both sunflower seeds and various other kinds of oil-bearing crops. We had an enterprising fellow travelling throughout the Soviet Union, who would send us all kinds of fat-containing crops. And so when someone from central office suggested that we should take on the processing of coconuts, purchased from the Americans in the Philippines, we jumped at the chance, because it would mean production at full capacity. They were bought, shipped to Vladivostok, and transported to us from there by rail. We were considered to be at the leading edge and to have highly appropriate personnel capable of coping with a completely new type of crop. We had to adapt the machinery and carry out a whole series of tests, and only after that were we in a position to begin to process the coconut.

'They sent us 2,000 tons of it. We took it in, found a place for it, set to work – at which point we were overtaken by the war. Well, the first day of the air raids on Leningrad – in my opinion, there are those who don't remember all of it, those who have forgotten it, and those who don't know exactly what went on. But I certainly remember it, because I found myself right in the thick of it. I remember that we were working under barracks conditions when the first air raid occurred. I don't know how much they dropped on the Badayev warehouses, but I know more or less precisely what was dropped on our factory, because all the "tail-ends" of the bombs, all the tail-planes were brought to me. Well, out of inexperience, we

54

rushed to extinguish the ones that we could see, that had fallen on the roofs (and these were wooden roofs), in the workshops, on the piles of coal that the boiler-room was burning at that time, simply those that had fallen on our territory. Naturally, the ones that had penetrated inside the bales of coconuts were not spotted – and it is possible that whoever was stationed near those warehouses was not sufficiently alert. I don't know what it was, but the fact is they only spotted it when all those bales with huge quantities of dry and fatty seeds (70 per cent fat, 2 per cent moisture) – when all that was set alight and such a fire began to blaze that it was visible from Krestovsky Island. That's the sort of fire it was. As I have already told you, we were utterly inexperienced. I was one of three at the factory who had a gun – see, I don't even know exactly what to call it – a rifle. I have to say that it's a real black mark in the story of my life because, as soon as they said that there were planes flying over our factories, we all rushed to put out the incendiary bombs and I stood the rifle in a corner somewhere – and it vanished! Can you imagine!'

'Tell me how you saved the oilcake from burning.'

'Ah yes, the oilcake. The warehouses were on fire, the copra was burning. Copra, of course, catches fire instantaneously. We had two rows of warehouses containing copra and, in between them, a building in which there were 800 tons of oilcake and, towards the end, when it had become clear that nothing could be done there, we decided to save at least that storehouse with the oilcake in it. And it was our director, Vasili Yakovlevich Trofimovsky – a really good man – who mainly put the fire out. I also grabbed a hose from one of the firemen (because he was being beaten well back from the fire – the blaze was incredible) and turned the hose on the storehouse. I hosed the director down too, when the overcoat he was wearing began to smoke. One of our workmen was standing on the roof – such a good chap – and he was also hosing down the fire. Someone was fetching water. And that was how we battled with the element of fire!'

'I believe the oilcake was later added to the bread?'

'Where did the oilcake go, you mean? I hesitate to say exactly.

But it was serving no useful purpose in our factory. The bakery next door – just over the fence from us – took it. That's where the oilcake went. Then they issued it as it was and as such the citizens availed themselves of it, ourselves included. And it certainly saved us from starvation, because we ground that oilcake up and it was our main source of food. We would heat it, make some kind of flat cakes out of it, and by that means we stayed alive. Of course, it wasn't just the oilcake that saved us. Our place was, after all, a fat-manufacturing business. We were able to heat it in grease of some kind and that's why there was never anyone who died of starvation at our place.'

Lidiya Okhapkina too had reason to remember the air raids of 8 September:

It was on 8 September in 1941. When the air-raid warning started up, I made a dash for the bomb shelter, but I didn't reach it in time, so I took cover in the entrance to a stone building. I stood there trembling with fear. A woman invited me into her place. She lived on the first floor. We had only just climbed the stairs and entered her apartment when we heard a deafening explosion, followed by an indescribable din and a flash of flame. The howling of engines deafened us all. The sound of bombs detonating boomed out somewhere quite close by. All the air, everything around was filled with cracking and whistling noises. Our building shuddered all over. It seemed as though the very ground was writhing in convulsions, like it does during an earthquake. My teeth were chattering with fear, my knees were trembling. I took refuge in a corner somewhere, clutching the children to me. They were sobbing with fear. I seemed to be losing consciousness from one moment to another. I thought that the end had come, that a bomb would fall on us any minute and we would all perish. We were all standing there like prisoners condemned to death. The woman whose apartment it was stood with her mouth open and her eyes wide, whispering something. Her mother, an old lady, had fallen to her knees and was crossing herself. And her children, a little bit older than mine, were also crying. We lived on Volkhov Prospect, not far from the railway line and very close to the front line. Because of this it was much more dangerous there than on Vasilievsky Island, for instance, or on the Vyborgskaya side, or on that side of the Neva in general. That air raid went on for a long time. I really thought that we would not survive it. After that night I found some grey hairs.

I made up my mind that we couldn't possibly go on living there any longer, all the more so because some buildings not far from ours had been demolished during the night. By morning they were smoking ruins. The girders stuck up like huge crosses over the people buried there.

I went over to the Petrogradskaya side to see Shura's wife, who was living not far from the Kirovsky Prospect. She had a little daughter too. I thought that we would get on well with one another, and what is more she lived on the ground floor which, at that time, was more convenient and safer. When I got there I told her the whole story. She agreed to take us in; the only problem was that, in order to stay there overnight, I had to obtain authorization from the militia. I had a long wait there.

I stayed at Inna's place for no more than two days. Her mother arrived from the suburbs, it became a tight squeeze for us all and her mother was not happy with the situation, so I left again and returned to our home in Volkhov Village.

Almost all the people living in our building had moved out. Some had been evacuated out of Leningrad, others had gone to live in the centre of the city with relatives or friends. The roof of our building had been set on fire, and there was no longer anyone living on the first floor. I lived on the ground floor, where there were two other families remaining. I lived in fear for the children, feeling like someone under sentence of death. Every time there was a bombing raid I expected to die. Then one day we received a visit from an official representing a District Council committee, who proposed moving us out to another region, saying that trams would be provided the following morning to transport all of us living in Volkhov Village. We were transferred to Vasilievsky Island where, through the good offices of the Vasilievsky Island District Council, we had been allocated a room, rather a narrow one – eight to nine metres square – on the island's first avenue, on the second floor, where from then on I did actually live with the children. This was around 20 to 23 September. The alerts and the air raids continued, and I would run with the children to the basement, where a bomb shelter had been constructed. But later on I stopped going there, because I was convinced that, if the building received a direct hit, no one would get out of there alive anyway. And besides the alerts used to begin well into the evening, between eight and ten o'clock, when the children had already fallen asleep, and it was difficult to gather them up. Tolya slept with his clothes on, as did I, even wearing his winter overcoat and his boots. He was difficult to pick up. On one occasion I had woken him up, to be able to run more quickly. He had only just got off to sleep and didn't want to get up at all. Through his tears he said to me: 'I don't want to go, let me die in my sleep, I won't feel any pain. I don't want to go, I don't want to go anywhere.' I found this unbearable to hear. From then on I stopped going down to the basement.

I no longer remember when it was that I washed the children. The public baths were operating only at infrequent intervals. And during the alerts it was dangerous to walk there. I decided to wash the children at home. When I undressed little Tolya, I saw that his body was completely covered with sores and scratches. He had impetigo, which he had picked up when he was away. I went to the chemist. There wasn't any impetigo ointment, so they gave me methylene blue. But before the ointment was applied, he had to be washed in water as hot as possible. On one occasion during this procedure – which was done at night – he was standing naked in the round washbasin and I was washing him with water so hot that I could hardly bear my hands in it. He was yelling. Suddenly there was an air-raid warning. There and then a burst of flame seemed to fly in through the window of our room. The old carpet that was serving as a curtain over the window fell down. The window smashed into smithereens. It all happened in an instant. And outside in the street I could hear deafening explosions. The children began to bawl loudly. I grabbed little Tolya first, naked and wet as he was, and almost flung him to the floor in the corridor. Then I ran for my daughter. I clasped them to me in a corner of the corridor somewhere. I was wondering when it would ever end, whether there would ever be an end to it. 'Monsters! Swine!' I cursed the Germans. In the morning, when I went to fetch the bread, I saw that half of the building opposite ours had been demolished. In the other half, still standing, the walls were covered with a whole variety of wallpapers: pink, blue, green, some with flowered patterns and some with stripes. And what seemed really strange – on one square of wall there was a big clock hanging and it was still going…

Returning now to Kniazev's diary:

16 September 1941. The 87th day. This is how it all happened.

In the morning I caught sight of detachments of armed sailors on the embankment. They were entering the doorways of apartment buildings. On the Neva opposite our building a naval supply ship was being unloaded. It turned out that they were setting up machine-gun posts in the windows of buildings overlooking the Neva. The sailors came into our building too, in order to install machine guns in the apartments of the Karpinskys, Sherbatsky, Pavlova and others. Immaculately dressed, really young sailors – cadets by the looks of them – were coming and going with sandbags in the darkness of the stairway. A full guard was formed up by the gates…

I went back home. What else could I do?

The building is being turned into a fortress or a pillbox. Will we be able to remain in it, even though our windows look out onto the courtyard? I don't mean now, of course, but in time of battle. But where is the enemy? A long way off? Close by? The sailors went about their business extremely speedily; even just crossing from place to place, they didn't walk, they ran. My wife and I have decided to move to the office temporarily. If we have to die, then let it be on duty, and not in some stairwell or bomb shelter. We gathered some essential things together, and a camp bed, and I set off for work.

Near the Academy of Arts I was struck by the fact that there were sailors digging small holes not very far apart from one another, placing something in them, laying bricks on top and strewing sand... Right up against the Sphinxes. It can't possibly be... My heart missed a beat.

Rain has been lashing down the whole day. The September wind is blowing. Somewhere in the distance the artillery batteries are clattering. In spite of the fact that it's not flying weather, there is the frequent drone of our aircraft's propellers. The whole city is bristling with bayonets, machine guns, firing points, obstructions. In some streets, in the approaches to the city, barricades are being erected. Leningrad has been got ready for fighting in the streets, in the squares, in the houses. What are we to be witnesses of? The hardest of days and hours are coming...

Night time. I am sitting in my study at work in the Archives. My wife is with me. She is having a nap on my camp bed. It is quiet. A darkened lamp is burning; it throws light only on this sheet of paper. In the corner the profile of a bust of Lenin shows up black against the white background of the wall. Would I ever have thought in the past that I would be obliged to spend the night in this cosy study under such exceptional circumstances? I am listening to the quietness, the alert has not sounded. As for my staff on duty – two are sleeping in the reading room, and one is keeping vigil in the room where the telephone is. It is black night in the courtyard. The pouring rain seems to have stopped. But there is a chill in the air and depression in the soul.

Belyavsky showed me a letter he had picked up in Zelenina Street near a destroyed building. A bomb blast had carried someone's correspondence and the pages of some manuscript out into the street... Can it be that the same thing will happen to my pages too?

'Tell me,' Belyavsky appealed to me, 'is it possible that there is no one currently keeping a written record of what is happening in the city, how people are living through events? How good it would be to organize such a record, to free a given person from other responsibilities, to commission him to go round the streets, to visit institutions, homes... Couldn't the Institute of Literature do this, for example?'

'No,' I answered. 'That would not come within its ambit. At the Institute they are literary historians and critics, not authors or social commentators....'

I didn't say a word about the fact that I, myself, am keeping such a written record anyway, as long as I have strength and time enough. It is true that my notes are limited to a very small circle and a restricted number of encounters and events. But probably there is someone else depicting events and experiences on a significantly larger canvas.

19 September 1941. The 90th day. I don't understand what is going on. On the 15th I had the impression that the enemy was expected in the streets of the city. I went to the Archives to spend the night, in order to share its fate. On the 16th I cheered up. Everyone was saying that the enemy had been driven off, our air force had been reinforced, the ring of encirclement was being broken from outside... On the 18th the illusion was brought to an end by an hour's heavy shelling of the city!

21 September 1941. The 92nd day. Three months of war. This last week, the 13th, was the hardest one for us Leningraders. I remember separate episodes now and, if I had not taken notes, I would not be able to establish from memory precisely what happened when. There are certain moments that are etched into your memory, as though with a red-hot branding iron, but it is not possible to determine immediately when exactly these occurred within a series of other events. Here are some of those impressive moments: the fire at the Senate building; the way our building gave a 'jump' up and down when two bombs were dropped; the whistle of artillery shells passing over the Archives; the dark bust of Lenin against the background of the dimly-lit wall of my study at work when I was spending the night there... Shakhmatova's glance when a shell flew past very, very close to her – silent and concentrated, but full of inner strength; the sailors running into the entrances to set up firing points, and many other moments too. They are all impressions of the past week. There are many of them, and they arrange themselves in the brain in such a strange way – not in chronological order, but according to some kind of capricious pattern.

What on earth is happening? None of us knows anything for sure. The enemy is at the gates. Somewhere near. But where? People look at one another in bewilderment, but rarely does anyone venture a question. In the newspapers banner headlines:

Fortify all the approaches to Leningrad. Transform each outpost, square, street and alley into bastions and fortresses and make them impregnable to the enemy...

Create fortifications that are unassailable by the enemy...

Leningraders have one and the same task to accomplish – to defend the city and annihilate the enemy...

All routes into the city must be barred to the enemy...

The enemy must expect death at every step and the destruction of his equipment.

The papers are full of quotations from the works of Lenin and other authors on how to wage civil war, build barricades, etc.

But the ring can only be broken from the outside and, if this does not happen, then the only thing left will be to die, defending our native city... The old workers of the Obukhovsky Plant are on record as saying: 'We have now only one choice: death or victory, freedom or slavery! Not a single step back... Conquer or die!'

Fearlessness in the face of death is being preached, cowardice and faint-heartedness mercilessly condemned. 'You won't elude death in this way. It will come just the same, only it will be a shameful death, to the sound of the jeers and taunts of the guards and executioners...' This piece of advice by General Cluseret of the French Commune is being quoted in the newspapers.

So, the apotheosis of an heroic death – this is the current slogan.

If we don't conquer, then we will die... There is nowhere to retreat any more!

An interesting comment made by a professor of mathematics, a specialist in probability theory, is going the rounds: each Leningrader has a 1 in 3 million chance of being killed or wounded. A completely insignificant value that can be ignored with tranquillity. But at the same time there was a single elephant present in Leningrad and it was precisely this one elephant that was killed in the course of a bombing raid on the city! So here you have probabilities with ratios of 1:3,000,000 and 1:1...

The newspapers are full of reports of German atrocities. If they were assembled systematically, you couldn't compile a more terrifying account.

22 September 1941. The 93rd day. My dear faraway friend, do you really need to know what my occasional reading is nowadays? If I were to lose my wife, see my city demolished and razed to the ground, the Archives entrusted to me destroyed, then what would I have to live for? But how would I end my life, if I were not killed? It would seem that hanging yourself is the best way, an ugly but certain death. So now I have taken down the encyclopaedic dictionary and I read: 'The noose, pulled tight by the weight of the hanging body, usually lies above the thyroid cartilage and, exerting pressure from front to back and from the sides, at the same time as blocking the windpipe, compresses the major blood vessels of the neck and the vagus nerve. As a result, complete loss of consciousness occurs instantly or in a few seconds, due to the lack of blood flow to the brain...'

But this is for the future, and in the meantime I am not losing either my presence of mind or my fortitude. I am carrying out my civic duties to the full in accordance with my position of responsibility.

8

The 100th Day of the War

From Kniazev's diary:

29 September 1941. Monday. The leaves are falling from the
trees, battered by the brisk September wind. Everywhere the wind
has blown drifts of sand over the asphalt. Sometimes the sky
clouds over, but then the sun breaks through with a bright flood of
sunbeams and illuminates our magnificent city with its brilliant
light. In these days when the city is undergoing such dreadful
ordeals, it has become more dear and more close even to those who
had grown used to it and had become indifferent. Each apartment
building, each street, each square, each alley – they are all so
beloved, so close to our hearts, and in such immediate danger!
Every day there are fires, buildings destroyed, people killed... Yet
people walk the streets, work in factories, in offices. They get to
work and confide in a low voice: 'We've had all our windows blown
out: the building next door was destroyed by a high-explosive
bomb. We will have to go to friends for the night.' And no one
knows how even this day that has barely begun – this bright
September day – will end.

   Evening. They have already been up twice from the Karpinskys'
apartment to warn us of imminent air raids. On the second
occasion, they said that they had heard a bomb come down
somewhere. I had got so tired during the day that I couldn't be
bothered to go downstairs... I am reading a book about world
history and writing these lines. But I'll make no secret of the fact

that, when the faintly perceptible trembling of the floor beneath your feet begins, caused by the vibrations created by aircraft flying close by, you can't help pricking up your ears and becoming painfully aware of these almost imperceptible tremors. You strain to hear whether the anti-aircraft guns are firing from the ships in the Neva. No, the window panes are not rattling, which means that enemy aircraft are not yet flying over the sector where we live. But we are ready all the same. I am sitting here wearing my cap and my galoshes, with my overcoat by my side. Just in case! And we are not sitting in the dining room but in the hallway, where there are no windows, only doors. Above us is the attic. We live on the top floor, the third, or, if you count the basement, the fourth. So you sometimes cast an involuntary glance at the ceiling.

By day, all these air raids and the artillery fire pass less noticeably. At work, neither I nor any of the others leave our workplace. I couldn't even chase out those of my staff who were not officially on duty on that ill-fated day when Leningrad came under fire from the long-range guns, and a part of the Senate building had already been set alight and was blazing brightly. But during the evening or at night, both the bombing and the shelling have to be endured under greater nervous strain. Yesterday, having seen the fires glowing, I didn't risk getting undressed for the night, but slept with all my clothes on, coming awake instantly at even the slightest shuddering of the building.

This is evidently how very many people live through these days and nights in Leningrad. At work today, a colleague told me that, after yesterday's bombing raids, she had found it hard to pull herself together so as not to strain her ears in the silence, to get to sleep. Many people spend their nights in the bomb shelters or else run to them whenever there is an air-raid warning. It is already a form of psychosis. Some people stay stoical and stubborn: fatalists, religious believers and people who are simply unmoved by anything; who are either extremely calm by nature or, quite the reverse, are in the extremes of exhaustion. Yesterday, during an alert, when we were standing on the embankment in the porch way of a building opposite St Isaac's Cathedral, there was one young woman who was reluctant to come in off the street, in spite of the insistent urgings of a militiaman.

'It's all one to me whether I live or die,' she said angrily. 'I'm fed up with everything, it's all hateful.' At that moment a coffin was carried past on a lorry, mourners with wreaths sitting around it. 'Now there goes a lucky man,' the woman said.

I couldn't contain myself and I asked her the question: 'Why are you so despondent, in such a low frame of mind?'

'I have lost two already and have totally lost track of the third: he was brought to Leningrad wounded, and I have no idea where they have put him.' She rattled off the answer. I put no further questions to her and, in any case, the all-clear had sounded. Everyone was leaping out of doorways and making a run for the trams waiting on the tracks.

There are others who have more stamina than that young woman, but there is a sense of dreadful weariness and extreme nervous tension... 'How long can this really go on for?' Petrova, a young mother, asked me. 'And what will happen afterwards? I've been calling in at one canteen after another. Finally, in one of them, I was given a ticket for the queue, a number in the seven hundreds. They told me that, towards evening, I would probably manage to get something to eat... It's already something to be thankful for that my baby isn't starving. I have received 500 roubles out of my husband's pay, but the money has stayed untouched, I can't find anything to buy with it. How on earth can we go on living? They say that Kronstadt has been bombed to the ground,' she added. She said all this calmly, without emotion. And as for another of my women colleagues, it is dreadful just to look at her. Her face is absolutely bloodless, emaciated. Today she heard that the postponed evacuation of mothers is being resumed once more, and horror is staring from her eyes again at the prospect of the ordeals of the unknown. It is hard here in Leningrad, but at least there is work and the canteen for academic staff and employees, where she takes her two children for their dinner. But ahead of her lies total uncertainty and heart-stopping fear for the fate of both her children and herself.

I tried to console both of them. I didn't downplay the threatening nature of events, but I pointed out that our situation was not a hopeless one. You just had not to let your willpower be overcome by despondency and distress. I must admit that they were only listening to me with one ear or, to be more precise, they were listening to me out of politeness.

One and all are facing the insistent and constant question: 'How long will this situation last?' Winter is coming. Added to all these trials and tribulations will be the cold. And for many people, even those with strong nerves, the unbidden question arises: 'Will we be able to hold out?'

To this question the women of Leningrad have given the unequivocal answer: 'Yes, we will!'

Yesterday there was a citywide women's meeting. Actresses, writers and workers took the floor. With one voice they called for the defence of Leningrad and pledged their fortitude and their support for the defenders. The whole assembly gave a standing ovation to one young woman, a member of a paramedic team, for having retrieved twenty-nine wounded fighters from forward positions while the fighting was going on. During this action she herself was wounded twice... Now that is genuine and blessed heroism!

I have purposely recorded my impressions within my small circle in such detail. How the whole of our existence, our life within the besieged city is full of contradictions. Anyone who talks about nothing but the weariness and depression will not be right; neither will the claim be true that there was nothing but undiluted heroism amongst the Leningraders. It was a life full of paradoxes. And it is the tip of it that I have attempted to depict in these pages.

5 October 1941. The 106th day. A little girl, Valya, who we were intending to take under our wing, called in. Their apartment building has been partly demolished by the shock wave from an explosion. The building next door was razed to the ground by an extremely powerful high-explosive bomb. All their simple furniture was shattered, the doors blown off, the windows gone, not just the window panes. This destruction took place at a time when she had gone to the trench digging with her mother (her mother had taken her along because there was no one to leave her with), which is how they stayed in one piece. Now they mostly live in the bomb shelter. They have nothing to eat, the mother has no job, they have only a dependant's ration card – that is to say, one that dooms them to starvation. Valya looks around with her fear-filled eyes and pricks up her ears: 'I think there must be an alert. I'll go to your courtyard and sit in the bomb shelter.' We checked and it turned out that there had been no air-raid warning. In spite of this, she was on pins and needles. We gave her some money, some food, whatever we could... Poor unfortunate child! What has she done to deserve such suffering?

6, 7 and 8 October 1941. The 107th, 108th and 109th days. Three very troubled days have passed. More precisely, anxious, nerve-racking days. Nothing in particular happened, everything went on in the same way, only there is a slightly different perception of the events that we have lived through. We are very ordinary people, nothing at all remarkable, and I have nothing that is in any way heroic to record. There is only one thing worthy of attention – the fact that we go on working all the time; even during the alerts at the office there is no interruption of the work. That is the only thing that must be ascribed to our 'heroism'. This, in essence, is what Leningraders are having to live through nowadays, and it is no small matter, either. I must give my colleagues credit where it is due: they are working quite well, in spite of the alerts, the cold, the malnutrition, the trying circumstances in the canteen, the semi-sleepless nights. Some are living with their windows blown out, others have been obliged to move in with acquaintances. In general, I am satisfied with my team. Not only are they doing their work, but they are also taking it in turns to stand watch in the evenings and at night, remaining at their posts during the air-raid alerts and the artillery fire.

9 October 1941. The 110th day. On the radio there was a broadcast by Professor K.F. Ogorodnikov, now serving in the Red

Army. He has a doctorate in mathematics, and has spent nineteen years in the laboratory studying questions relating to the structure of the celestial vault, observing the heavenly bodies through the telescope. Now he has joined the ranks of the Red Army as a volunteer and has learned how to shoot a rifle and hurl hand grenades. He said: 'I have many students, many friends and acquaintances. I want them all to know that their professor and colleague – Red Army soldier Ogorodnikov – will be steadfast and brave, as befits a Soviet soldier, when he engages the enemy in combat.'

The professor then addressed himself in English to his colleagues in friendly Great Britain. He passed on greetings to Sir Spencer Jones, the Astronomer Royal, and to Professor Smart, with whom he shared a bond of many years of joint research in the realms of astronomy.

10 October 1941. The 111th day. I have been working all evening on my history of the Academy of Sciences. It is now around midnight. A student has called in on us three times, to tell us about the air-raid warnings. I am sitting in the hallway wearing my overcoat. It is cold. We are beginning to be on the alert. There is sporadic firing from the anti-aircraft guns. I have set aside the cards with the rough notes for my history of the Academy. I am listening involuntarily for the rumble of the guns and I take out some paper on which to note down my impressions of the day.

16 October 1941. The 117th day. Grave news again from the Viazma and Kalinin areas. It is clear that the enemy forces, conclusively and catastrophically as far as we are concerned, have broken through our line of defence outside Moscow. A sense of alarm has overwhelmed all of us. Our homeland is in mortal danger.

20 October 1941. The 121st day. The radio started up at six in the morning. A state of siege has been declared in Moscow. For any kind of breach of public order, for spreading provocative rumours – shot on the spot! On the approaches to Moscow, the town of

Maloyaroslavets is constantly changing hands. In 1812 this long-suffering town was passed from the Russians to the French and back again ten times! The situation on the Moscow Front has obviously deteriorated disastrously.

21 October 1941. The 122nd day. The Leningrad food situation is worsening. For the second ten-day period in October, dependants were on a bread ration of 200 grams, received 100 grams of meat, 200 grams of cereal, 100 grams of fish products, 50 grams of sugar, 100 grams of confectionery and 100 grams of vegetable oil. Office workers and children received a little more. Factory workers, however, were on rations twice that of office workers. There is nothing that you can buy with money, and so it is losing its value. Those who have plenty of money don't know what to do with it, and are either buying all sorts of rubbish (expensive perfumes and the like) or (those who are more practical) are buying up all the manufactured goods remaining in the shops to use for barter, once money has lost all its value. Of all the future trials facing Leningraders, starvation is almost the most terrifying. Starvation and bombing! All we need to complete the picture would be an outbreak of cholera, or plague, or simply typhus, the famine fever. You have to discipline yourself to look events straight in the eye and think about the future as little as possible. Time enough to ponder over it when the future actually arrives!

Today Filimonov, our all-purpose handyman, paid us a visit. 'It is hard to work', he said, 'when you have grown weak through lack of food. In the Academy canteen for the second day running, apart from soup, there was nothing but boiled rye macaroni.'

It appears that a bomb dropped by the vultures between five and six o'clock the other day, falling in the Moika, was an exceptionally powerful one. It was undoubtedly intended for the General Staff building. It landed not far from the house containing Pushkin's last apartment.

22 October 1941. The 123rd day. It is night or, more precisely, morning: it will soon be dawn. For the time being we Leningraders, forgetting our own woes, have turned all our thoughts towards Moscow, the heart of our Soviet homeland. How could it have come about that the enemy has crushed our armies and infiltrated the most vital centre of our country? This is the persistent, agonizing question. The enemy, equipped with the most modern and advanced military technology and with all the achievements of science at his disposition, has turned all this to destruction, to annihilation, in fulfilment of the predatory designs of the conqueror, the tyrant. He destroys all cultural values that lie in his path, like an untamed barbarian, some kind of vandal, a Hun, only 100 times more ruthless. The barbarians had no scientific expertise, no technology. They were simply two-legged beasts of prey. The German invaders are two-legged beasts of prey, but highly sophisticated ones!

Hitler has now concentrated all his forces outside Moscow and flung his reserves into combat too. How could anyone sleep peacefully on such a night as this, when the most bloody battle in world history is being fought for Moscow, for the integrity and the very existence of our homeland?

They say that in one of his speeches Hitler threatened to wipe Moscow off the face of the earth, as the breeding-ground of the Red contagion. That was four months ago and, at the time, seemed monstrously boastful, ridiculous... And now, in these grim October days, his armies are at the gates of Moscow!

23 October 1941. The 124th day. An overcast day. Rainy. Yet people are enjoying it more than they ever enjoyed warmth and sunshine: 'It's not a day for flying, there won't be any bombing.'

At my office in the Archives, hunger has somewhat disrupted the work. One colleague in particular has succumbed: she is truly very unwell. She sits in Room 12, near the toilet, where a little stove has been installed, and smokes, smokes endlessly. And coughs.

We are taking all possible steps to protect the Archives from the cold during the winter. But only one room is to be heated. Today I could barely sit it out in a temperature of two degrees above freezing.

This morning I rode along past the beds that had been freshly dug for future flowers and I was touched once more – living beings are getting on with the business of life!

9

The End of Childhood

Returning now to Yura's diary:

5 October 1941. Now I will describe what happened last night. There were about eight alerts during the night. They were absolutely terrifying. Several times the whistling of a bomb was so loud that I felt sure it would fall on the school. At precisely one in the morning I relieved Finkelstein in the observation post. Up till then, no alert! The first half-hour passed peacefully. Then suddenly the silence was ruptured by a whistling noise, then another... then another. Flash, crash! Flash, crash! I jumped off the table I had been sitting on and peered gingerly out of the window of the observation post. There were about ten incendiary bombs smouldering in the schoolyard and on the neighbouring buildings. I immediately gave three rings to alert the third observation post. Later it turned out that I had been slightly mistaken to do so – a bomb had fallen beside the school wall, in the yard, where the third observation post was. Well, it goes without saying that all the bombs were swiftly extinguished. Then the Germans dropped several high-explosive bombs as well and only after that was the air torn by the mournful sound of the siren. At my post all was calm. But, beginning with that one, the alerts were not normal. The anti-aircraft guns were completely silent. All you could hear was the distant droning of the aircraft, the sound alternately swelling and fading, and now and then a piercing whistle – then the screech and the impact of an explosion. The night was an extremely anxious one for me. I didn't sleep a wink. Still, that's the kind of nights Leningrad is getting nowadays.

6 October 1941. Nine in the evening. An alert. Anfissa Nikolaievna and I are at home. Anfissa and her family have been allotted a room in our apartment. Mother and Ira have gone downstairs. We have received a letter from Tina. As of 2 October she was alive and well. She writes that they are under bombardment. Just hints at it, of course. She worries about us.

At school lessons have started up for the tenth-year classes. I asked my teacher to give me some mathematics homework. She did so.

8 October 1941. I went for a thorough medical examination. It turned out to be a good job I did. I didn't pass the medical because of my eyesight. I have 20 per cent vision in my left eye and 40 per cent in my right. What a blow! Mother insists on immediate treatment. I will probably have to wear glasses. Volodya Nikitin went in for his medical straight after me. He will most likely pass it. But the main thing is, I did pass the orthopaedic and the ear-nose-and-throat parts of the medical.

Mother has forbidden me to read. So as not to hurt my eyes.

9 October 1941. It is half-past seven now. An alert has been announced. The sky is almost cloudless. The situation on the various fronts is as follows: according to the official communiqué, Orel has been taken and the Germans are launching an offensive against Viazma and several other cities. According to rumour, the Germans have been driven not less than sixty kilometres away from Leningrad.

11 and 12 October 1941. Nothing special has happened. Mother and Ira are downstairs and I am at home. It is half-past seven.

There is a rumour circulating at our school that the Germans have decided to put an end to the war before winter sets in, and have mounted a really large-scale attack on Moscow. According to Finkelstein, Nikitin has not passed the admission examination.

Mind you, with the father he's got, he'll get into Cadet School just the same.

Igor, Anfissa Nikolaievna's brother, has promised to procure a top-category ration card for us. I don't know whether it will actually happen.

Roll on lesson time! This is boring.

13 October 1941. The day passed off peacefully. To make up for it, the night really made itself felt. In the evening I learned something very interesting from Mother. She had run into an acquaintance of hers, who is now working in a hospital. They are offering me a job at this hospital. I would be responsible for escorting patients from one hospital to another. I would have sole responsibility for their safe delivery. If I were to lose one of them, I would find myself facing a criminal charge. I would travel around at night, usually in a vehicle. I would be paid a salary of twenty roubles a month and given a worker's ration card. Dinner might be included. I would work one day on and one day off. I agreed. Needs must...

I saw Volodya Nikitin. He has been accepted into the Cadet School. He starts his classes on 15 October.

My initial opinion of the night was that it looked fairly promising. Clouds in the sky, a certain amount of fog – would any aircraft take off on a bombing raid? But... at five minutes to seven they announced an alert.

The first and second observation posts were being manned by myself, Dodya, Boris and a couple of women. Dodya and I were sitting on the steps. Oh, those endless, anxious nights! They will remain in my memory for ever. Semi-darkness, in front of me a hurricane lamp in a bucket, the staircase and a window to one side, anti-aircraft guns thundering out their fire, ears pricked to catch the slightest sound, heart beating wildly at the loud whistling of a bomb, senses keenly alert on hearing the whine of a German plane. The window is constantly being lit up by flashes from the explosions, and every now and then the staircase and the whole building shudder and tremble from the impact of a high-explosive bomb dropping nearby. And so it goes on, night after night. You long to sleep, to eat, to be oblivious to it all, but then something whistles past your ears again, you instinctively press yourself against the wall and hunch your head down into your shoulders... and the whistling dies away. Then a flash lights up the window, the staircase shudders, and only after that does the distant rumble of the explosion reach you.

It had been more or less peaceful last night, and Dodya and I had gone up onto the roof. We had barely had time to look around when searchlights appeared in the sky and, without any warning at all, a bomb began its furious hissing, getting louder and louder. Dodya and I were in the attic in less time than it takes to tell, not feeling the bruises caused by the drop. Realizing that it would be dangerous for us to stay in the attic, we started down towards the stairs and at that precise moment there was a brief whistling sound followed by explosions above our heads. It became brighter than day. Dodya understood what it was before I did and, grabbing a shovel, rushed to extinguish a bomb. I did too. A crazy race against time began. We were working in dense, acrid smoke that seeped into our throats, irritating them, penetrating into our very lungs; sweat was pouring down our faces, but we kept on dealing with the bombs. I ran over to the first observation post. There was some woman standing there, shouting out in terror: 'A bomb! Put it out!' She was scraping up sand in her cupped hands and throwing it onto the burning fragments of thermite. I grabbed a shovel and in no time at all had strewn sand over everything alight. Bright light gave way to deep darkness. Having got out of the attic somehow, leading the woman by the hand, I ran over to the second observation post. There all the bombs had already been extinguished. I glanced out over the roof – there were about ten people milling about on it. I wanted to breathe in some fresh air, to come to, to pull myself together. Soon the all-clear sounded. After that, nothing new happened. There was one more alert, but it posed no danger to us. When it was over, Finkelstein and I fell fast asleep and slept till morning. The radio woke us up, broadcasting bad news: Viazma has fallen. The German offensive is continuing.

76

Later on I discovered that twenty-three bombs had fallen on our school. (I had extinguished two and helped to extinguish a third.)

14 October 1941. An ugly scene at home today. Ira threw a fit, on the grounds that I had eaten in the company canteen and she hadn't even had a bowl of soup there. Mother told her to calm down. At the same time she told me that Ira had been offered some beetroot soup at the canteen and some beans with pork fat, but Ira had insisted that they made her sick, and had refused to eat them. She had eaten the remaining half a bar of chocolate, and that was it. She refuses to eat and she takes it out on me! 'I have to go hungry!' she says. But who is standing in the way of her eating? Mother has already begun to tell me that we must get used to the idea that if a man is fed a bowl of soup a day, he should be satisfied with that. But suppose I can't get used to such an idea? I don't eat even a half, a quarter of the amount I need to feel full. Oh, this war, this war!

It is dismal, overcast weather at the moment. There is a frost and light snow is falling.

15 and 16 October 1941. Nothing special has been happening. Dodya and I didn't go to school today, but went to the theatre together to see *Dangerous Corner* by J.B. Priestley. An extraordinarily good thing. A wonderful stage setting, on the whole an excellent piece, but, unfortunately, rather like a huge vaudeville production. But I liked it so much that I ranked it alongside *An Ideal Husband*.

This evening during a night-time alert I extinguished an incendiary bomb in the courtyard, prevented the log pile from going up in flames, and the whole building as well.

The situation on the front lines is disastrous. According to the latest communiqué, Mariupol has been taken, an offensive has been launched against Kalinin and, as matters stand, the western sector of the Front has been broken through! Nowadays, whenever I look towards the future, my hair stands on end: chemical warfare, winter, German oppression: it's all a bit too much. Or, death in the front line, death by bombing, being maimed – but somehow I carry on.

17 October 1941. I have committed a dreadful crime: I have lost the key to our apartment. What on earth will Mother say when she gets home tonight? I had been to the eye clinic. The doctor there sees patients from nine in the morning until one o'clock, every day except Friday. On Fridays he sees people from two in the afternoon. I had also been to the photographer's, to have a passport photo taken. I feel sure it will turn out ugly, because my hair had flopped all over my forehead.

Yesterday there was an unpleasant scene involving our room neighbours. When Anfissa's husband got home, he accused her of smoking. (For those with tuberculosis, smoking means a slow, certain death.) He began to shout at the top of his voice, without being the least bit concerned that he could be heard. She seemed to be arguing the toss with him, while he went on shouting very rapidly: 'No, no, no! Liar! Liar! Liar!' Then, when the air-raid warning went, he got ready to go to the bomb shelter and began to drag her with him. She didn't want to go. Then he snatched the handbag containing their room-key out of her hands and began to make off. She caught up with him, clutched at the handbag, and a brief tussle took place. And all this before our very eyes! Afterwards there were other, similar scenes, but I'm not writing about all that here. She is his second wife – he divorced the first one. But I don't envy her the life she leads even though she's well fed. I would sacrifice all my modest amount of food, just not to be insulted like that.

The situation on the front lines is appalling. The Western Front has been penetrated, the German assault troops are creeping towards Moscow, throwing a ring around our forces. The German air force is bombing Leningrad every day. At night. The same thing is undoubtedly happening to Moscow, Kharkov, and so on. The whole of the Urals is blacked out and there is a rumour that Ufa has been bombed.

I asked Igor about the situation at the Front today. He said that

Moscow is in imminent danger. Leningrad has been completely cut off from the rest of the USSR. The situation at the Leningrad Front is so-so: they are holding on. In Leningrad the reserves of food are coming to an end. Apparently, deaths by starvation will soon follow, epidemics, etc. I dwell with anguish on the fact that I didn't get evacuated. Nowadays I'm afraid even to look ahead – you live one day at a time.

Tomorrow at school I am going to resign from night fire-watching duty because I have nothing warm to put on my feet. Now would be quite the wrong moment to catch a cold.

I have continual stomach cramps from hunger and there is a steady flow of saliva. And this is in spite of the fact that I ate in the company canteen today. Lack of bread is the first thing to make itself felt. Today Mother bought some little spice cakes made from oatmeal and a small amount of sugar. They are good made like that. I would consent to live on such a ration for some time, for three years even, provided they didn't reduce the ration, but that is actually bound to happen.

18 and 19 October 1941. Mother took two days off work. She intended to go after some potatoes, but the problem solved itself differently. Some cabbages were delivered to the local public dining room – a whole lorry load of them. And so all the residents of our apartment building made a beeline for them. Each took as much as he could. Khabidulin took about forty cabbages for himself, but we only took about ten, because there was only Ira to carry them. The next day we ate cabbage until it was coming out of our ears. The night passed off peacefully.

The situation at the Front is extremely grave.

They say that we will start school again on 25 October. But I don't think it will happen.

In the last communiqué we were informed that the city of Odessa had been evacuated over the course of eight days.

I have now ventured a glance at the future. If the German offensive is beaten off, then everything will be fine. We will have won the war. If the offensive is merely brought to a halt, however, then it will mean lengthy starvation for us. If the Germans succeed in taking Moscow, then for us – death.

20 October 1941. In the morning I was at a loose end. I walked for a while in search of *kvass*, got chilled to the bone and returned home. It was freezing cold at home. I kept my overcoat on. I got something to eat from the company canteen: cabbage soup and beetroot. I ate, sat for a while, then went over to Mother's place. I borrowed some books by Voltaire and Dumas from the library there. I ate my dinner in their canteen. I had some oatmeal soup, then I went home. There was an alert as soon as I got there. I read some of the Voltaire. Igor looked in. He said he would bring the ration card during the evening, but I don't believe in it any more. In the shops they are not giving out anything yet for the third ten-day period of the month.

Later that evening, Anfissa told Mother that Igor wouldn't be able to give us the promised ration card after all.

10

The Situation Worsens

Returning to Kniazev's diary:

26 October 1941. The 127th day. While I was climbing the stairs to our apartment, a neighbour who had overtaken me asked me: 'Well, since you are the great optimist, what is your opinion about Moscow? Will we win or will we abandon her?' My answer was roughly as follows: 'The situation is obviously extremely grave. A decisive battle is taking place outside Moscow, where all the enemy's forces and our own are concentrated. But no matter how it turns out, I am absolutely convinced that Germany will not conquer us. We have manpower resources on our side as well as the inexhaustible material resources of the United States and England, battling against Nazi Germany. It is a fight to the death that is going on, with no possibility of a peace compromise. And at the end of the day Germany will be defeated. This conviction is the mainspring of my cheerfulness and my optimism.'

My neighbour smiled, but said nothing in reply.

On the radio they are playing the *Internationale*. The day has ended. It is midnight. Tonight we will go to bed without undressing.

This is how it is in my own small world. But what is going on in Moscow? My heart bleeds at the thought of the ordeals that have befallen the Muscovites. A decisive battle is being waged and the Muscovites are in the thick of it. I am gripped with horror at this idea. Is it possible that the most brutal trial threatens our homeland?

Better not to dwell on the future. We don't have any future. But our homeland does!

Perhaps it is because I am the director and behave severely and don't take part in conversations about wartime issues or the difficulties of survival, but for several days now I have not spoken to anyone about the events we are enduring. My colleagues are keeping their heads down – not a word from anyone about current events...

It took a big effort, but I managed to get my colleagues started on their work again. We now all sit together in one room – the reading room – where a little stove has been installed. We stoke it with all kinds of rubbish, as well as paper. It is relatively warm, around eight degrees above freezing! We can get on with our work!

29 October 1941. The 130th day. Two alerts during the evening.

It is becoming increasingly difficult from the food standpoint. Today's dinner was absolutely sparse. But it is tedious to write about it. So far, there are only shortages, not yet starvation. We can put up with it. We must.

31 October 1941. The 132nd day. We are in the grip of fear as it is, and the newspapers are stirring things up, scaring us, quoting Hitler's pronouncements: 'Starting from now, the extermination of 20 million people will be one of the basic missions of German policy, a mission planned for long-term implementation. We must first of all expel and eliminate the Slavic peoples. A natural instinct commands every living being, not only to defeat his enemy, but also to exterminate him. In times past it was recognized that victors were fully within their rights to annihilate tribes and even whole nations. We are faced with the task of decreasing the size of an alien population, as well as with the duty of furthering the growth in numbers of the German population. We need to develop the technology for the reduction of the alien population.'

And there are several column inches of newspaper comment on this declaration. On reading all this, even a man with nerves of steel would feel a cold shudder begin to run through him. Could there ever have been a more sombre period in the world since the beginning of civilization? Most probably not. There was cruelty, but it was due to savagery. Now there is a refined cruelty of the mind, a perverse and purposeful technology, a science of destruction.

1 November 1941. The 133rd day. The last part of the journey home has to be travelled under artillery fire. Academician Krachkovsky and his wife were following along the embankment behind me, calmly, at their normal pace. My wife greeted me joyfully, with relief in her heart: 'Ah, there you are, you got here – I was beginning to get worried.' The shelling couldn't be heard indoors, but the building would give just its usual shudder.

There were two air-raid warnings during the evening. And now the depressing music of the wailing siren lingers in my ears.

We dined extremely frugally. On this occasion, to make matters worse, I very much wanted to eat.

I am finding it difficult to cope with my inner trepidation about the total lack of future prospects. On top of that, the protection of the Archives troubles me greatly. Today I did the rounds of the entire storage area and issued a whole series of instructions. Little by little my colleagues are giving in. One of them, who looks gloomy enough anyway, is lashing out at everyone with a sick bad temper. I even asked him whether he was feeling unwell. Another has become completely glassy-eyed, and a third has retreated into a profound silence. One woman has got down to her work again, but gazes around with unseeing eyes. Whatever she is thinking as she lives through what is happening, she hides inside herself – she never speaks out. And I have suddenly become fed up, alone in this roomful of people who are somehow ebbing away within themselves.

7 November 1941. The 139th day of the war. Throughout the day they have been broadcasting speeches and music over the radio.

I listened to yet another broadcast from Moscow, a speech given by Stalin during the parade in Red Square. Apparently, tradition remained unbroken and the parade began at nine o'clock in the morning, although rather a special one this year. The troops moving across Red Square were either heading for the firing line or were returning from there for a rest period, straight from combat.

Stalin has been silent for a long time, then suddenly there have been two speeches in a row. It feels like some sort of turning-point in the war situation. The Germans are hurling all their forces at us, all their reserves, but we are no longer in retreat. There is nowhere to go! It's either die or stand up for Moscow and Leningrad. There is no third solution.

Dreadful news has appeared fleetingly in the newspapers. Knut Hamsun, an outstanding Norwegian writer, having reached the conclusion that it was impossible for Norway to survive as an independent country, has gone over to the side of the Quislings, which means full collaboration with the National Socialists.

In a leading article in the *Leningrad Pravda* they are saying: 'We have sacrificed a great deal, but the ultimate sacrifice – that of letting Moscow go – we will never make.'

The war will demand yet greater sacrifices and over a long period. Stalin says that we must not just exaggerate the strength of the enemy, nor the obstacles to victory, the way some gutless intellectuals do.

Ahead of us lies war, nothing but war until we have totally worn the enemy down. Nothing else, just war.

They are shelling again!

12 November 1941. The 144th day. Now hunger is not merely knocking on the door, but has come right inside on its bony legs.

The food situation in Leningrad is precarious. They have been announcing this over the radio and in the newspapers: 'Bolsheviks do not hide the truth from the people.' It is a difficult situation. It will not improve until the siege has been lifted. From tomorrow onwards the standard issue of bread is being reduced – not just for the civilian population, but for the troops as well. The question being raised by the faint-hearted about the possibility of surrendering the city 'to the mercy of the enemy' cannot be contemplated. Leningrad must defend itself, whatever the outcome might be. There can be no talk of surrender! We must bear all the burdens and ordeals that have fallen to our lot, including hunger.

My wife and I have calmly faced up to this next stage in our lives. Either we endure, or we die. But it is better not to think about the future. Let that future come, and then we will have to surmount it.

The Germans intend to starve us out. Will the Leningraders, nearly 3 million of them, be able to endure this immense ordeal? But it is not just a question of starvation. It was good flying weather today and there were five alerts in the course of the day. During the final long air raid of the evening, we again felt the building sway. The whole building shifted. It means that a bomb had fallen nearby. And evidently not just one. When we felt the building move, my wife and I got to our feet, then we sat down again and began to drink our evening tea. In the morning there was artillery fire. So we have hunger, cold, bombing, and shells whistling over our heads.

My wife says: 'We will endure everything, provided the Germans are driven out.'

16 November 1941. The 148th day. Early in the morning we attempted to wash ourselves and put on clean linen. We couldn't manage it: coming one after another, the air-raid warnings forced us to remain on the alert. We started to tidy away all the things in the room that might fly about – a screen, pictures, vases, a mirror and so on. The apartment has begun to look like a shed.

The shelling began promptly at four o'clock, as if they were working to a timetable. We had draped extra pieces of old cloth over the windows so that, in the event of a shock wave, the shards of glass would not scatter too far. I took the lamp in my study off the table and set it in a corner; I placed the clock from the mantelpiece alongside the wall. There is a box of sand standing almost in the centre of the room, and a can and bucket of water by the fireplace.

In spite of the bitter weather, our next-door neighbours' windows are open; the floor is littered with bricks, clay and cement; the whole floor is filthy and there is a layer of brick dust over everything. For three days workers have been constructing machine-gun nests in the windows looking out over the embankment. All the neighbours' belongings have been moved, everything turned upside-down. Needless to say, you can't live in rooms in such a state. They have arranged to live in the kitchen, where the windows look out over the courtyard.

Before long, by the looks of it, we too will be obliged to move out of our apartment. I don't regret anything, except the books and these notes of mine, and the accumulation of materials and collections. But perhaps, even before that, we will be bombed out or burnt to death.

17 November 1941. The 149th day of the war. Should I take my notes on any further? They are taking on the extremely monotonous aspect of a catalogue of the destruction caused by the enemy air raids. As a contemporary, I cannot get a real grip on events and my ambit is too restricted to permit a full and varied description of them. I am trying to broaden my horizon to include general information, gleaned from the newspapers, but should I need to do this? I don't really take upon myself the role of historian or war correspondent, or something of the sort, when I write these jottings.

There again – should I be writing about myself, about my own experiences? I might seem to be showing off: 'look at our hero, stoically and courageously enduring all these ordeals!' Indeed, I do endure them stoically, but I endure them from a dialectical standpoint, and there is much that is contradictory...

3 December 1941. The 165th day of the war. There has been no electricity all evening. It is hard to write with just the little oil lamp.

Today at work we got very little done. There was a great deal of agitation on account of the proposed evacuation. We had received an official notification about it in the morning. Orbeli and Urmancheieva who each have three children are keen to leave;

Travina is vacillating. The remainder have refused. The journey would involve going on foot for about 150-200 kilometres. They are promising to provide transportation for the luggage and the children. A panic-stricken fear of death by starvation is pushing people to take enormous risks. Orbeli said: 'It's an even choice: starve to death here, or leave and have at least some chance of being saved.' She had brought all three of her little girls to work. I looked at them and thought about the coming great exodus of long-suffering Leningraders. They will have to travel through the freezing winter nights of December or January, in intense cold, through blizzards and snowdrifts, over trackless wastes. A desperate gamble.

5 December 1941. The 167th day of the war. Today is Constitution Day. The trams are running decked out in red flags, but for some reason there are no flags hanging from the buildings.

Again, like in 1919 and 1920, I encountered in the street a coffin being dragged along on a sled. An aged mother and her son were found dead in their apartment, the latter wounded and driven out of his mind in the war with Finland, relatives of Valya, the little girl we wanted to look after. They had to break the door down to get in.

8 December 1941. The 170th day of the war. It is evening. It is impossible to get anything done with the little oil lamp. I am burning a candle. After that, let come what may! The blessings of civilization have come to an end, or are coming to an end with brief intermissions.

My wife said: 'If it's going to go on like this, we are bound to die of starvation in January or February.' She said this unemotionally and added: 'But since death by starvation is extremely agonizing, we ought to find some other way to die. You will kill me, and then yourself as well...'

And it was my wife who was saying this, my vivacious and loving wife and companion!'

11

The Ice-bound Sphinxes

Kniazev's diary continues:

12 and 13 December 1941. The 174th and 175th days of the war. Today my proud Sphinxes looked to me like wretched naked puppies, abandoned in the brutal freezing weather. It's as though everyone had forgotten about them. But there they stand, above the white expanse of the Neva...

Yesterday, on arriving home, it was impossible to linger under the portico of our building: shells were bursting on the far side of the Neva; today they were crashing down every single minute, somewhere farther away. I walked for a while between the columns. For some reason there are fewer pedestrians there. Many are in search of an evacuation point and become fretful when they find no such thing; others enquire where the social security department is. These are the invalids. Some can barely move through old age or from debility. It is painful to watch these human remnants. Along the embankment piled high with snow a path has been cleared, to create a thoroughfare. But it is only a rare vehicle that travels through, evidently on some special detachment or in use by the medical service.

When I am walking or standing still by the columns, I can invariably see what is quite a commonplace scene nowadays: two or three people dragging on a little 'funeral sled' an empty coffin that they have bought, hastily knocked together, unpainted, or one with the deceased already inside.

They say that many such coffins are piling up at the cemeteries.

From our columns the Nikolaievsky Bridge is in plain view. The wires on it have been partly torn away, the trams can't go across it. And only the unending black files of pedestrians are moving in both directions. My Sphinxes are jutting out lonely amid the snowdrifts, and in front of them there is a lorry with no front wheels. It has been standing there for three weeks. Perhaps it was hit by a shell, perhaps it was involved in an accident – I don't know. But evidently there is no one to remove it, or they have no time. And this broken-down machinery is standing in front of the watchdogs of thousands of years – the Sphinxes from Ancient Thebes in Egypt.

I close the porch doors behind me. The glass panes of the outer one have been boarded up with plywood, those of the inner one have been shattered by shock waves from the explosions, one of them just recently. It is dark in the stairway and no one has swept it for more than a month: cigarette-ends, papers, sand and dust are lying there... Whenever anyone is going out, we call out to one another, so as to leave room. Indoors we are living in the hallway. For the second week running there is no electricity.

At work it is hard with several colleagues growing weaker. There is frost in the storage rooms, in the rooms where we work as well. The electricity goes off constantly, and then the staff are left sitting in semi-darkness. It is pitch-dark on the stairs then. There is no way we can keep the door onto the street locked. You can't hear anyone knock, and the door-bell doesn't work without electricity. Several other colleagues and I are occupying one of the protruding towers adjacent to the Zoological Institute, where it had been relatively warm, but now it has become extremely cold there too. Today I got thoroughly chilled there, but I sat it out for five hours, working on a history of the chairmanship of academic departments.

I have purposely dwelt at such length on the details of our everyday life within my small circle. It is hardly likely that anyone else will be writing about it at present. Life at the Front itself, the life of heroes, will be illuminated to a sufficient extent by others.

Of us only one thing is required – to survive, to endure, to last out until the turning-point, until victory…

And already there come glad tidings from around Moscow about a new blow inflicted on the enemy. Hitler himself has announced that he would be postponing the taking of Moscow until the spring. Our winter is not to the Germans' liking. Oh, if only they would all freeze to death outside Moscow, outside Leningrad, in the Ukraine, if only their lines of communication would be severed by gigantic drifts of snow! Let the accursed vandals disappear, who forced their way into our land, daily bombarded the streets, the squares, the apartment buildings of Leningrad! Let them disappear without trace! Perhaps the rout of the German armies has begun already? Let their machinery break down in our snowy wastes! And then the vandals would have to accept retribution for the dreadful crimes committed. They will not remain unpunished…

I am finishing my notes. I am watching my little flickering lights with terror – the stock of fuel is running low. Can it be that soon I too will have to live in darkness morning, noon and night, groping my way about?

17 and 18 December 1941. The 179th and 180th days of the war. At the Front our troops are inflicting blow after blow on the German invaders. Sectors of the Northern rail network around Leningrad occupied by them (from Tikhvin as far as Volkhov) have been cleared. The Octyabrskaya railway line is being cleared. Only the Murmansk line is firmly in the grip of Finnish-German troops, based in Petrozavodsk. A mass of goods for Leningrad has accumulated in Murmansk. This news is being passed from mouth to mouth; weakened, exhausted people are gathering their strength.

But there are many who are already beyond recovery. Yesterday near our academic building, near my frequently-mentioned columns, a man died. The manager of our building, Savchenko, saw a woman take the man by the arm to cross the road. The latter could barely walk, he collapsed near the tramlines; she raised him up a bit, and he followed on for a few more steps, but he couldn't reach the pavement. He fell beside a pile of snow. When Savchenko approached him, he could already see that the man was dead. The woman, his wife, was fussing over the dead man. Bystanders, realizing what was the matter, advised the woman not to let on that she was his wife, but to behave as though she were a stranger. That way the militia would be obliged to take the body and deal with it in the proper way. Which is just how it happened. A patrolling militiaman stopped a passing sledge, and they loaded the body onto it for conveying to the mortuary. What became of the woman, losing her husband and not even being able to bury him, I don't know.

Savchenko himself looks on with such a melancholy gaze: 'Well, you have to die, you can't hold out.'

'No, you don't have to,' I assured him. 'We will endure, provided we don't lose the will to overcome obstacles.' I also told him at length that we had to hold out, not give in to fear. Apparently this had an effect.

It turns out that there is no one on watch in our building. No one is going up to the attic. When I started to speak about the instructions for extinguishing incendiary bombs during winter conditions, printed in *Pravda*, he merely smiled sadly: 'Who on earth would there be to do it? No one has the strength; out of the caretakers, Alexander is lying down, all swollen up, and the other one, Starikov, has become very weak... There is no one left in our building to carry out such instructions.'

So, we are now living at the mercy of the will of circumstance.

At work, too, it is difficult to arrange for defence. There is no one there to carry out the instructions either.

It is dismal in the storage rooms and in the freezing-cold rooms where we work. In a fit of depression, I think: 'Why are we sitting here? Why aren't we working at a factory bench, making the sorts of things that they need right now at the Front?' As far as I'm concerned, at the moment I am finishing off the work for a lecture entitled: 'Towards a history of chairmanship at the Academy of Sciences throughout the period of its existence.' All that, of course, could easily wait.

A great many people have left, either of their own accord or through cutbacks at the various city establishments and enterprises, and so there is always someone from the family on duty in the queue... It means that there are so many people not being made use of at all for defence. Is it possible that in the spring these people will not apply themselves to growing vegetables, catching fish, etc? I always think with regret that, so close to the Neva, only a few kilometres away there is Lake Ladoga with its fish, but even in peacetime we existed here without fish! Truly, half Russia could have been fed with the fish from our region's thousands of lakes! It never happened! And now, with supply so difficult, Leningraders are swollen with hunger and are dying.

This evening someone began to bang on our door insistently. We were obliged to open up. In staggered Filimonov, a joiner and jack-of-all-trades, but never really finding his feet in academic institutions. He normally occupied the post of odd-job man. He was a big drinker. He was jovial a little while ago when he repaired a crutch for me and wanted food for it, not money. Today he was a terrifying sight, hair all over the place, black in the face. He was holding a lighted candle in his hands, and he sank down onto his knees with it: 'Save me! I am done for, I have lost my ration cards, give me some bread!' My wife went into a spin. What were we to do? Give him our own daily ration, namely 125 grams? But that would truly not have saved him! How and with what could we help him? I pulled out thirty roubles and gave them to him – the price of 100 grams of bread in the marketplace. Filimonov took the money, assuring us that it was bitter, hard, awful for him to beg.

This unexpected visit in such a dramatic atmosphere completely put us off our stroke for a while. Later on I calmed down. I could never bring myself to beg in a time of such hardship. Everyone is in exactly the same plight. And if death was inevitable, then I would find within me the willpower to do away with myself.

The candle is burning down – a Christmas candle from my wife's reserves. We bought a dozen for Christmas three years ago. They have come in wonderfully handy! It will soon be Christmas. It is likely to be the dreariest and most frightful one of the past 2,000 years. But here in the USSR we got out of the habit of observing this festival a long time ago. One of these days it will be more worthwhile for such a festival to take place, an annual event in the life of our planet. Earth, having withdrawn to its maximum distance from the Sun, must approach it again. It would make a fine celebration of the return of the Sun!

12

I Dream of Bread

Yura's diary continues:

21 October 1941. I was on duty at school from eight in the morning until six in the evening. Still, I did manage to take the edge off my hunger today. Or, rather, I drowned it out.

An unpleasant conversation about food again in the evening. Hunger is no kindly aunt...

Mother bought the week's allowance of sweets on her ration card – 150 grams – and gave it to Anfissa Nikolaievna (she owed it to her). The latter just thanked her and took it absolutely calmly. Now all we have left at our disposal for the ten days of the ration period are just six or eight little sweets! You can bet your boots they won't be there tomorrow!

On the various fronts the situation is grim. As if we hadn't enough to cope with, fighting has broken out in the Taganrog direction. Is it possible that we will be unable to defeat the German assault troops and won't be able to restore communication between Leningrad and the rest of the USSR before 1942?

If only I could be sure that they won't reduce our rations for food and bread any further! If only I could be sure! But they will reduce them. They will reduce them at least twice more. And this will happen just before the October anniversary, the anniversary of the greatest proletarian revolution in history, which took place on 25 October!

It turns out that there are many books on chess in the school library, amongst them *Modern Opening Gambits*.

22 October 1941. I hung about in queues for beer all morning. With great difficulty I obtained two bottles; my feet were frozen. Then I redeemed three coupons for cereal. In the evening I was on duty at school. There were no air-raid alerts. Taganrog has been taken by the Germans. The German offensive continues...

I have been engrossed in reading a novel by Alexandre Dumas: *La Dame de Monsoreau*. A fascinating story.

Mother has exchanged the two bottles of beer for 400 grams of bread. I am being sent off to the beer queue again.

23 October 1941. I got two more bottles of beer. I went to the cinema and saw *The Festival of Saint Jorgen*. I read *La Dame de Monsoreau*.

At home we have both cold and hunger. Both at the same time.

24 October 1941. I spent the whole day from ten in the morning until six in the evening in the queue for beer, instead of reporting for duty at school. There was not even time to stand in line for a passport at the militia post. And, in spite of all that, I didn't manage to get any beer. Mother came home in the evening and used up another head of cabbage. One way or another I managed to take the edge off my appetite. There was nothing of particular interest in the news bulletins. Mother told me that the Trade Unions' Central Committee has been evacuated to Kuibyshev. I can just imagine the situation in Moscow.

They are giving out a monthly tea ration of twelve and a half grams per person; eggs are not being given out at all. Nor fish. Anfissa Nikolaievna's behaviour was of interest today. She gave us three carrot fritters made from mashed carrot that she got from her canteen, and ten sweets. So there was something to have with half a mug of tea. I wrote a letter to Tina. I asked her to send us a parcel with dried bread or potato patties in it. I must give some thought to getting a job. I will have to forget about studying for the time being.

Something strange is happening to Ira: during the day and in the evening she has blue blotches under her eyes, if she moves quickly she gets a stitch in her left side, and she can't eat liquid food (soup). Mother intends to take her to see a doctor.

What now? What kind of a surprise are the Germans preparing for us? In any case, the Germans are threatening to burn Leningrad to the ground in the course of three days of non-stop air raids. (This rumour comes via the Chistovs who, when working in the outskirts, couldn't avoid reading the propaganda leaflets dropped by the Germans.)

There are queues everywhere: for beer, for *kvass*, for fizzy water. For pepper, for salt (especially for salt!), for mustard.

The Germans have either switched all their air raids to the Moscow Front or else they are getting ready to bomb us on the anniversary of the October Revolution. They want to turn our shining holiday into a day of mourning. I found out only today that I had been commended for extinguishing incendiary bombs in the attic and the courtyard of our building. I don't even remember any more when that was.

25 October 1941. All I got from standing in the queues was frozen feet. I didn't get anything else.

Oh, how I long to sleep, sleep, eat, eat, eat! Sleep and eat, sleep and eat... What more does a person need? But if a person was well-fed and healthy, he would soon find something else to want, and so on indefinitely. A month ago I wanted – or, rather, I was dreaming about – bread with butter and sausage, but now I just dream of bread itself.

Tina sent us two more postal orders in a row: for 200 roubles and 210 roubles. They have probably given her another stripe, perhaps even two: she's been made Army Doctor First Rank. That's probably what it is.

For the second time in a row I am skipping fire-watching duty at school and the day after tomorrow (assuming I am still alive and well), I will have to skip one more. But who could ever have suspected that events would turn out like this? If I try to look ahead, my hair stands on end: cold, hunger, shelling, bombing, sleepless nights and exhausting days, without any let-up, then come chemical weapons. Those who survive the first day of their use will die of starvation: all the food in the shops will be contaminated. I am not looking any further ahead: to remain in Leningrad from now on is a sentence of death.

Mother tells me that now is not the moment to be keeping a diary. But I will keep it. If I don't get to re-read it; someone else will re-read it, will learn that there was such a person in the world as Yura Riabinkin, will make fun of this person... For some reason a phrase from Gorky's *Life of Klim Samgin* came into my head: 'But perhaps there was no such boy at all?' A person existed – a person is no more. There is a folk riddle that asks: 'What is the shortest thing in the world?' And the answer goes: 'Human life'. I might take up philosophy one of these days. But to do so now I would need: 1) food and 2) sleep. This also explains all idealism: for idealism to exist, it must have a basis of materialism.

26 October 1941. There is plenty of money about, but starvation is here just the same.

29 October 1941. I am now so weak that I can hardly make my legs work, and climbing the stairs is a huge effort for me. Mother says that my face is beginning to swell up. This evening Anfissa Nikolaievna let drop an interesting observation: 'People are all egoists at the moment. Nobody thinks about tomorrow, so everybody eats as much as they can today.' She is right, this plump pussycat.

Today I wrote another letter to Tina. I have asked her to send a parcel of potato patties, oilcake and so on. Is it possible that such a parcel would be out of the question? I ought to get used to going hungry, but I can't. What am I to do?

I don't know if I can go on studying. The other day I intended to get on with my algebra, but there were no formulae in my head, just loaves of bread.

This would be an appropriate moment for me to re-read Jack London's short story *Love of Life*. A wonderful piece, and nothing could be better for my current mood. They say that all the rations will stay the same on the ration cards for November. Not even bread has been increased. Mother told me that, even if the Germans were beaten off, the rations would stay the same.

The Germans will probably announce a non-stop bombardment for 7 and 8 November. But in the meantime they will be tormenting the population all they want with their artillery fire and bombing. They are planning a holiday surprise for us.

These days I am not taking much care of myself. I sleep with my clothes on, I just splash my face slightly once a morning, I don't wash my hands with soap, I don't change my clothes. It is cold and dark in our apartment; we spend the evenings by candlelight.

But what I find the most offensive, what is absolutely the worst thing for me, is that here I am, living in hunger, in cold, amongst fleas, while there is a room next door where life is completely different, where there is always bread, porridge, meat, sweets, warmth, a bright Estonian oil lamp, comfort. The name for what I feel when I think about Anfissa Nikolaievna is envy, but I can't overcome it.

I have no one I could go to. To my comrades? I have none. Vovka is in Kazan. Mishka is at work. There are others, but deep down they are egoists at heart, so what should I go to them for? But envy stirs in me again, anger even, and the most bitter resentment.

31 October and 1 November 1941. What can I say about these days? Anyway, I felt incomparably better on the 31st than I had done before. Aunt Natasha treated me to some mustard flavoured fritters, and even Anfissa Nikolaievna gave us 150 grams of cereal.

Tonight there was an alert. The anti-aircraft guns were in action, but the Germans dropped no bombs. During both these two days the guns have been keeping up a ceaseless shelling of the city. Anfissa's husband said the Germans have moved up their long-range artillery from the English Channel to Leningrad. Today, 1 November, I had an unpleasant and humiliating experience: they would not allow me to enter the company canteen before two o'clock. And by two o'clock the canteen had run out of mashed potato and I had to be content with two bowls of lentil soup. I bought three little bottles of cough syrup. It is a mixture of rum, valerian, and some drops of a Danish remedy. It is an extraordinarily sweet and nourishing potion: I have already drunk two bottles of it and have one left.

3, 4, 5 November 1941. On each of these three days lessons have been held at school. The requirements have been lowered, and only a few of the original teaching staff have remained. The rest have come from School 213. The school canteen has begun to operate. Soup without ration cards – one bowl per person – but everything else on ration cards.

There was an alert each night. Bombing. Yesterday three German aircraft were shot down over the centre of the city during the night. The shelling goes on all the time. And, on top of that, we have the holiday ahead of us. What sort of a 'holiday' will the Germans present us with? Chemical weapons, for sure. For the next four days, starting from 6 or 7 November, all the decontamination centres in the city have been placed on high alert. What on earth is going to happen?

We were supposed to have read Gogol's *Dead Souls* for school today, but it is impossible to read in the dim candlelight. Writing you can do automatically. I haven't heard much news. They are saying that the twenty-fourth anniversary of the revolution will settle everything...

What is man and what is human life? What are they, when all is said and done? There is an old saying that runs: 'Life is just a kopeck'. How many people lived before our time and how many of them had to die? But it is good to die, feeling and knowing that you have achieved everything that you dreamt of in your childhood and youth, good to die knowing that you will be succeeded by your scientific or literary works, but it is still so hard to do... What is Hitler hoping for at the moment? The creation of his empire, the very concept of which will be cursed by mankind in days to come? And so, because of a handful of desperadoes, millions and millions

99

of people are dying. And these are people! People!

It is late by now. The shelling has died down for a while. The candle is guttering. Hunger, cold, darkness, filth, lice, and the prospect of a crimson future, wrapped in a dark shroud.

6 and 7 November 1941. I have no idea what the situation is on the various fronts. They say that Stalin made a speech and that he explained the reasons for our retreat in the speech, and it stood out that he referred harshly to the USA and to England, saying that their help at the moment was negligible and that we were effectively fighting against Germany on our own. I ought to get to know this speech in greater detail.

Lessons are continuing at school, but there is something I dislike about them. We sit at our desks in our winter overcoats; many of the children completely ignore their homework. In the literature classes, it is of interest to note that children speak of the characters in *Dead Souls* in the words of the textbook where they are presented. Some of them have never even read *Dead Souls* at all.

Apparently, we have no more rice left. That means that for the coming three days I will be sitting here utterly starving. If I survive, I will hardly be able to drag myself about. I have switched to water again. I will swell up, but so what? Mother has fallen ill. And no laughing matter, once she herself had admitted being ill. Symptoms of a cold, coughing and retching, wheezing, high temperature, aching head… It seems that I must have been taken ill as well. The same high temperature, headache, cold symptoms. All this is most likely due to the fact that, when I was on duty at school, I had to go across three courtyards without a coat or hat. And this was happening in the middle of the night, in a severe frost.

For some reason studies are reluctant to enter my head at the moment. I have absolutely no desire to study at all. The only thoughts occupying my head are ones about food and about the bombing and shelling. Yesterday I picked up a basket of rubbish, took it down to the courtyard, and could barely climb back up to our second floor. I was as tired as if I had been hauling about thirty kilos for half an hour, or so it seemed to me. I sat down and could hardly catch my breath. There is an alert on at the moment. The anti-aircraft batteries are firing full tilt. A few bombs have fallen as well. According to the clock it is five to five in the evening. Mother should be home shortly after six.

13

Nearing the Limit

Yura's diary continues:

9 and 10 November 1941. When I am falling asleep I always see bread, butter, pies and potatoes in my dreams. And, as well as that, before sleep comes, there is the thought that in twelve hours' time the night will be over and you will have a piece of bread to eat. Mother repeats to me every day that she and Ira have only two glasses of hot, sweetened tea and half a bowl of soup during the day. Nothing more. And then a bowl of soup in the evening. Ira has even been known to refuse an extra helping of soup in the evening. They both keep telling me that I eat like a worker, meaning that I have two bowls of soup in canteens and that I eat more bread than they do.

These days my whole nature seems somehow to have changed abruptly. I have become sluggish, feeble, my hand trembles when I write, and when I walk my knees are so weak that it seems to me that if I took another step it would be the last, and I would fall down.

If I didn't have well-fed people around me, I am absolutely sure that I would have got used to all this by now. But when every sound you hear speaks to you of something cheerful, something satisfying... When I am sitting in the kitchen, I am faced with the sight of a pan left on the stove with the uneaten remains of dinners, suppers and breakfasts, left there by Anfissa Nikolaievna, and I can't stand it any longer. I am being torn to pieces – I don't mean

102

literally, of course – but that's what it feels like. And the smell of bread, pancakes and porridge tickles my nostrils, as if to say: 'Look, here it is! Here it is! You're starving hungry, but it's not for you!' I have got used to the shelling, I have got used to the bombing, but I can't get used to this – I simply can't!

On the various fronts the situation remains unchanged. It is only in the Kalinin direction that our detachments have moved forward a few kilometres. The enemy is stubbornly determined not to surrender his positions around Leningrad.

Again today my ear was struck by Anfissa Nikolaievna's cheerful laugh. Yesterday Mother borrowed a piece of sugar from her and today she intends to borrow another from the Kozhinskys. But today is the last day of the current ten-day ration period, so tomorrow we will have sugar of our own and bread as well. Bread as well! Only one night to go...

We haven't been able to buy our full rations in this ten-day period: we are due 400 grams of cereal, 615 grams of butter and 100 grams of flour – but these items are nowhere to be found. And where they do come on sale, huge queues form, hundreds and hundreds of people out in the street, in the bitter cold, and the amount delivered is usually just about enough for 80 to 100 people. So people stand there, get chilled to the bone, and leave with nothing to show for it. People get up at four in the morning, queue outside the shops until nine in the evening, and still come away with nothing. It is killing, but there is nothing that you can do about it. At the moment there is an air-raid alert in force. It has already lasted for about two hours. Need and hunger drive people out to the shops, in the freezing cold, to join the long queue, the crush of people. You only have to spend a few weeks like this to find that you have absolutely no desires left. All that remains is a dull, cold indifference to everything going on around you. You don't get enough to eat, you don't get enough sleep, you are cold and, on top of all that, you are expected to study. I can't do it. Let Mother solve the problem of what I should be doing. And if she is incapable of doing so, I'll try to do it instead. And what does the evening hold in store for me? Mother and Ira come home, hungry, frozen and tired. They can barely drag themselves along. There is no food in the house, there is no firewood for the stove. And then come the raised voices, the insinuations: how is it that the people who live downstairs managed to get cereal and meat, but I did not? There was meat to be had in the shops, but I didn't get any. And Mother flings her arms wide, puts on an innocent expression, and says plaintively: 'Well, I'm busy too, you know. I've got a job to do. I can't go and get it.' So I have to go and queue again, and all to no avail. I realize that I am the only one who can fetch the food that brings all three of us back to life. But I don't have enough strength, enough energy to do it. Oh, if only I had a pair of felt boots! But I haven't. And each time I stand in a queue, it brings me closer to pleurisy, to illness…

I am sitting here crying. I'm only sixteen years old, you know! What bastards they are to have brought this whole war down on our heads!

Farewell, childish dreams! You will never again return to me. I will avoid you like madness, like the plague. Let all the past be swallowed up into hell, so that I won't know what bread is, what sausage is! So that I won't be haunted by thoughts of past happiness! Happiness! There is no other word to describe my previous life. Being able to view my future calmly! What a feeling! I will never experience it again…

How I wish that Tina could take my diary and read it through in her room in Schlüsselburg, over a cup of tea and a sandwich. Never in her life has she had to go through what we in Leningrad are going through now.

After the alert this evening I went to the shop in Sennaya Square. In hand-to-hand fighting in a huge crush of people – such a crush that grown-ups were shouting, moaning, sobbing – I managed at the cost of incredible physical effort to squeeze myself in, to get inside the shop, having jumped the queue, and to get 190 grams of butter and 500 grams of sausage made from horsemeat and soya. When I got home, I felt an intense pain in my chest, exactly like the one I had two years ago. I am undoubtedly having a dry pleurisy attack. The pain is acute, the same in every respect as what I had

Georgi Alexeievich Kniazev. Photo taken in 1945.

Lidiya Georgievna Okhapkina with her son Tolya. Photo taken in 1940.

A Sphinx and a bronze lantern in front of the Academy of Arts.

Yura Riabinkin. Photo taken in 1939.

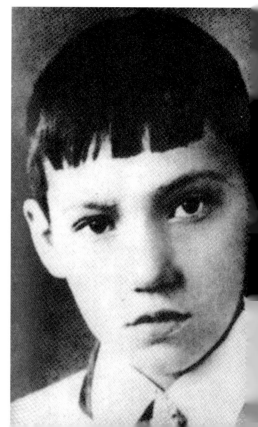

Тетя Даша на посту.
Пост—на Энском чердаке.

Даша смотрит в высоту,
Клещи стиснула в руке.

A poster showing 'Aunty Dasha' fighting with incendiary bombs.

'There are always four, five or ten people standing by the display board'. (*From Kniazev's diary*)

Women and children leaving the city.

Evacuation on foot.

One of Leningrad's central streets after a bombing raid.

Destruction on the outskirts of the city.

Clearing the streets of snow.

Unloading the snow that has been cleared from the streets during another snowstorm.

A body being taken for burial by sled.

The vegetable garden beside St. Isaac's Cathedral.

Young Leningraders 'digging for victory'.

Mourning for a baby at a cemetery.

An anti-aircraft emplacement beside the Bronze Horseman.

Nevsky Prospect after bombardment.

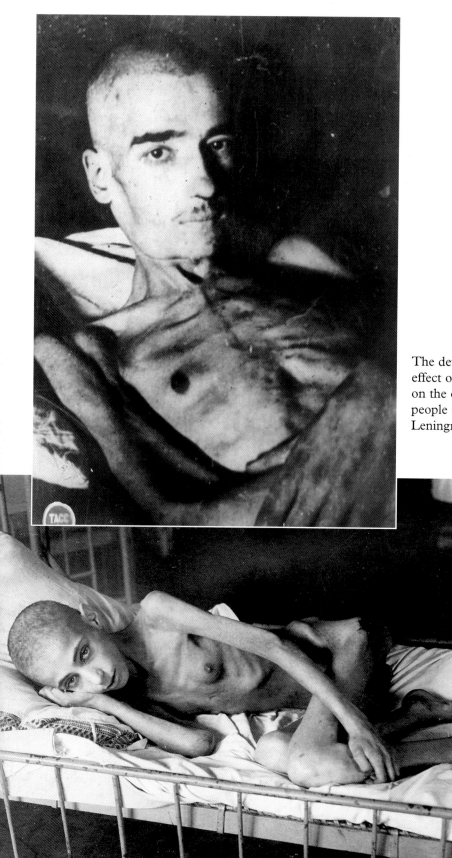

The devastating
effect of the siege
on the ordinary
people of
Leningrad.

Even young children worked during the siege.

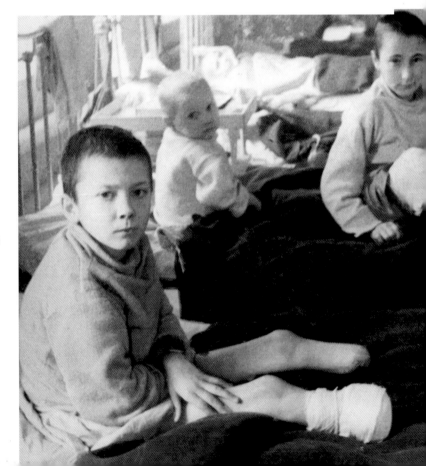

Injured youngsters
at a children's
hospital.

Tanks rolling to the front.

First-aid workers in action.

A Little Hawk ('Yastrebok,' Soviet aircraft) in flight over the city.

A battleship in the Neva.

'For the beginning of the Red Army offensive in summer 1943'.

A tank under the Arch of the General Staff building.

The Mariinsky (Kirov) opera and ballet theatre after bombing.

Soviet troops entering the city.

Greeting the Red Army with flowers and smiles.

The fireworks to celebrate the ending of the siege.

before. What torture! Tomorrow I will go to the tuberculosis clinic without fail. When it comes down to it, I don't want to die of pleurisy here and now. What can I do about it? What? I am powerless. There are only two effective means to combat pleurisy: 1) excellent food with plenty of fats and 2) a dry, clean, warm atmosphere. And both of these means are lacking...

Mother and Ira have had 'breakfast' and have gone to work. I will go to the tuberculosis clinic. However, before that, I will have breakfast in 'comfort and cosiness'. I will read for a bit...

Today I got four litres of beer on the ration cards and gave it to Anfissa Nikolaievna. She gave me half a litre of it back to drink. I enjoyed it. Truly, if these were the old days, I would have become a dedicated alcoholic!

Oh, I forgot to mention a most important thing. Mother's legs have swollen up and become as hard as stone. What a do!

I shall have to go to the tuberculosis clinic tomorrow, the one where Anfissa Nikolaievna goes. It is near the Maltsevsky market-place, which comes under shellfire every day.

They are quoting this order of Hitler's in the *Leningrad Pravda*:

'Taking into consideration the importance of coming events, in particular the winter and the poor supply of materials to the troops, I order that, at whatever cost, the Bolshevik capital Moscow be wiped out with minimum delay.'

I must get to the queue by five in the morning without fail. We are all overstrained. I haven't heard calm words from Mother for a long time. Whatever topic she touches on in conversation leads to swearing, shouting, hysterics, or something of the kind. The reason? There are many reasons, among them hunger and the ever-lasting fear of the shelling and the bombing. In our family – which consists of just three people – there is constant bickering, serious quarrelling. When Mother shares something out, Ira and I watch like hawks, to make sure she does it accurately. It's a bit embar-rassing to write such things down.

Meanwhile, at Lake Ladoga, an intensified inspection of the ice was under way. They tested the ice every day. Eventually, on 17

November, it was possible to step out onto the ice. The lake had iced over, although not totally. It was a stroke of luck that it had happened so early. The surveyors ventured cautiously out over this first thin sheet, which was still flexing beneath their feet. They had lifebelts over their shoulders, stout poles in their hands. They reached Kabona safely.

The following morning, 18 November, they went out onto the ice again, marking the route of the road to the mainland. Water traffic had ceased and, as if out of spite, the weather was no good for flying either. The cargo planes were unable to deliver to the city even that small share of supplies that they had airlifted in before.

On 19 November the surveyors and the road engineers prepared the ice route, which had to be cleared of snow and ice hummocks and have any cracks covered over. The hard frost, roundly cursed by the Leningraders, was welcomed with open arms there, because the harder it froze, the faster the ice formed. By 20 November it was already eighteen inches thick in some places. More than 300 horse-drawn sledges slid down onto the lake and began to head for the mainland to pick up flour.

More from Yura's diary:

24 November 1941. How wearily the time drags! It is so monotonous. All my thoughts are preoccupied with food and the desire to break free from the grip of starvation, cold and fear. All hopes of being evacuated have been postponed indefinitely. The Germans have once more seized the initiative on the various fronts and outside Leningrad. They have clearly moved even closer, since their shells are exploding in our street, in front of our building.

I was standing in queues today from half-past six in the morning. Endless lines, endless files of starving people – they will be etched in my memory for ever! I didn't get anything. In no shop was there any butter, cereal or meat. Not in a single one. And I spent a whole four hours queuing outside the shops. And I have to get back into the queue again.

Mother says that, firstly, the Northern railway line has already been cleared and is now under reconstruction (it had been dismantled), and, secondly, that there are many signs pointing to the evacuation of all State organizations and other similar enterprises. Mother is muttering something unintelligible about being evacuated but, judging by appearances, it won't come off.

25 November 1941. I visited the eye doctor today. He prescribed glasses for me, saying that I have no vision at all in one eye and 30 per cent vision in the other. I think that I had better go to a private clinic.

On the Southern Front some units have assumed the offensive and driven the Germans back sixty kilometres, wiping out a rifle corps.

Around Ufa bread costs two roubles and fifty kopecks, as much as you like and without ration cards, and the people there reckon that is expensive. How do you like that, eh? A real paradise on earth.

26 November 1941. From early this morning the city has been under severe shellfire, particularly in the vicinity of Sennaya Square and our own residential area. Building 30 was hit by two more shells. There were many dead and wounded.

Today Shtakelberg's mother called me a complete idiot for not stealing food from our room neighbours. 'I would,' she said, 'I wouldn't think twice.'

Instead of vegetable oil they are giving out jam. I stood in the queue. Oh, if only I could get some coconut fat somewhere! Anywhere!

Mother has filled in an application form for her to be allocated a place on a plane flying out of Leningrad. My feeling is that it won't come to anything, and although I nurse a secret hope of being freed, I am still oppressed by a number of negative thoughts.

Mother has demanded Ira's bread ration card back from me. They want to deprive me of my biscuits. Well, let them. Once Ira gets her hands on the biscuits, she will cling to them so hard that I will never see them again. And the rotten, ugly scenes over sharing out the food will start up again: she got less, she wants more...

107

Well, let's see, I'll still be able to get some biscuits tomorrow, but, starting from the day after tomorrow, my life – which is not very attractive as matters stand – might as well end. What kind of life would it be, deprived of biscuits? So, let them do the shopping now, get some potato flour and coconut oil or jam, and they will be complaining every day about how tired they are, and so on. Ira will be clutching the biscuits with both hands.

The situation hasn't changed in the least. The offensive against Moscow is continuing. Tula has fallen. There is fierce fighting going on in the Tikhvin area. There are persistent rumours running around that, as soon as the German army has broken through, it will immediately be pulled out of Leningrad and thrown at Moscow, while Leningrad will be surrendered and the citizens allowed to retreat on foot along with our army. What a bad mood I'm in! What black thoughts!

Meanwhile the troops and the sailors of the Baltic Fleet were doing everything in their power to equip the road over Lake Ladoga properly, to provide lines of communication, supply transport and set up repair facilities. Special units were moved up to the lake: anti-aircraft batteries, fighter planes, detachments of sappers and engineers, and medical teams.

On 22 November 1941 the ice route was tested. Later it became known as 'The Road of Life'. During the first weeks of its existence it was barely functioning. Only convoys of sledges crept cautiously over the thin ice. Later on the first lorries set off, but they frequently broke down. Transporting the cargo to the lake had its difficulties too: on 8 November the Germans occupied Tikhvin and the last railway line through Vologda, Cherepovets, Tikhvin and Volkhov was cut. It was only in December, when the troops of the Volkhov Front freed Tikhvin, that it became feasible to rebuild the railway line and extend it right up to the eastern shore of Lake Ladoga. It was then possible to deliver cargo directly to the ice road.

Until then, in September and October 1941, the tiny Ladoga fleet (a few tugs, motor boats and barges) had been tackling a task that was well beyond its capabilities: delivering supplies of food, shells, ammunition, fuel and lubricating oil to Leningrad, and evacuating people from there. It turned out to be a stormy autumn, so the crossings were often suspended. Then, during the last quarter of October, such a swell got up that water traffic ceased completely. Up until 20 November 1941, only isolated vessels got through to Leningrad. The delivery of food by air was also cancelled: the battle for Moscow was in progress and Stalin had ordered all aircraft to be deployed on military operations.

Returning to Yura's diary:

28 November 1941. I have been to the tuberculosis clinic. I was sent to have an X-ray done and some samples taken for analysis. I don't know what is supposed to happen next.

Today I am going to beg Mother on bended knee to let me have Ira's bread ration card. I will throw myself to the ground and if she refuses me even after that... well, I won't have the strength to drag myself about any more. Today the daytime air-raid alert has lasted somewhere in the region of three hours again. The shops are all shut, so where can I go to get potato flour and jam? When the all-clear sounds I will go out and scout around. As for being evacuated, I have given up hope. All that is just talk. I shall abandon my school work – I just can't get it to go into my head. And how could it? At home there is nothing but hunger, cold, quarrels, tears – with well-fed people living alongside. Each day is quite amazingly similar to the previous one with regard to its monotony, its thoughts, its hunger, its bombing and its shelling. Now the electricity has been turned off, and somewhere I can hear an aeroplane droning, the anti-aircraft batteries are firing, and just a moment ago our apartment building shuddered from the shock wave caused by a bomb exploding nearby. The weather is dull and grey, with dense white low-hanging clouds; the courtyard is full of snow, and my heart is heavy with thoughts just as ugly and grey. Thoughts about food, about warmth, about comfort. Not only is there not so much as a crust of bread in the house (the daily bread ration is now 125 grams per person), there is not even a crumb, nothing at all that could be eaten. And it is so cold, your hands freeze, your feet get frozen...

Today, when Mother comes home, she will take Ira's bread ration card away from me. Well, let it be, I will give it up for Ira's sake, so that she at least will stay alive in all this hell and, as for me, I will manage somehow. If only I could get out of here! If only I could get out! How self-centred I am! I am getting callous. What has happened to me? The day before yesterday I scraped food out of Anfissa Nikolaievna's pan with a spoon, I furtively stole butter and cabbage from the hidden reserves for this ration period, I watched greedily how Mother divided a sweet into pieces for Ira and me, and I pick a quarrel over every little fragment of food, each tiny crumb. What has happened to me? I feel that, to turn myself back into what I used to be, there would have to be hope, the conviction that tomorrow or the day after my family and I will be evacuated – that would be enough for me, but it won't happen. There won't be any evacuation. And yet, deep in my heart, a secret flicker of hope lingers. If it were not for that, I would steal, rob – I don't know how far I would go. The one thing I wouldn't go so far as – I would never become a traitor. That I know for certain. But as for all the rest...

I can't write any longer: my hand is frozen stiff.

29 November 1941. Two news items yesterday. The first was a letter from Tina, written on her way to Siberia in the town of Bui, where my grandfather died of typhus during the time of the Civil War. She writes that the situation is satisfactory (which means good), that she is going far, far away. The letter was written towards the end of October. The second news item was that Mother has decided to get out of Leningrad, come what may. Even if it has to be on foot. But this is still just a matter of words. I have to go back to school again, because only registered students are allowed to be evacuated out of Leningrad. Incidentally, I will have to pay 100 roubles towards my schooling.

Personally, I find the situation in Leningrad very hard to bear. The lack of food, the ceaseless shelling of all areas of the city, and much more besides. But, in general, I believe that the situation as regards evacuation is beginning to be more or less sorted out, although getting it completely sorted out will still take another month to a month and a half.

I am selecting what to take with me. I have firmly made up my mind to take with me, if at all possible, a school satchel with my various bits and pieces in it: two books on chess, a small amount of English literature, the *History of Diplomacy*, several historical maps, the cream of my postcard collection, two or three of the textbooks for the ninth class (for instance: *Fundamentals of Darwinism*, and the textbooks for literature, history and geography — or perhaps not that last one).

It is very nice to lose yourself in sweet dreams, like that of being evacuated, but the cold brings you back to reality with a bump.

I am staggered by the change in Anfissa Nikolaievna's behaviour. Yesterday, for example, she gave us a plate of millet porridge and a saucer of dried bread, without taking anything for it. She often used to bring cocoa powder from the company canteen, but that has now disappeared. Today I managed to get some jam for her and she gave me fifty grams of it back. On the whole, I have a real sense of her support nowadays. If we lived side by side for another six months, we would probably become good friends. However, who really knows her? The fact of the matter is that one of these days she won't be around in Leningrad any more. It is late now, evening. We ate some fruit soup made from potato flour and the jam that I got today, together with the dried bread that Anfissa Nikolaievna had given us, also with jam.

Tomorrow Ira will get 250 grams of biscuits on her ration card. What a lot, eh? Well, so what, let her eat the lot!

Today Mother said that she had applied for a permit to leave the city by air. Who knows what will come of it? Let's hope for the best.

A stormy scene took place in Anfissa Nikolaievna's room. Her husband picked a quarrel with her because she barters bread for vodka for herself, and so on.

So, that's it for 29 November. I didn't write much this evening. I felt like going to bed, but I didn't fancy going out into the cold corridor. And I long for something to eat. Another week of this and I won't be able to drag myself about.

30 November 1941. My mother is clearly in the mood for evacuation. She had a long conversation about evacuation with Anfissa Nikolaievna yesterday. The latter gave her – or, to be more precise, promised to give her – the address of her parents, who live in Zlatoust. Although it is not even a grain-producing region, the level of hunger there is probably nothing like what it is here. But everything depends on the decision reached regarding Mother's application. That much is clear. The answer has to be given not later than a week from now.

Anfissa Nikolaievna gives us about eight pieces of dried bread every day. Today she also gave us a piece of horsemeat and a bottle of vegetable oil. I am truly grateful to her for all this.

At noon on the dot the Germans launched another air raid. Again, they were simultaneously bombarding the city from the air and shelling it from their gun emplacements.

I am beginning to save money. I now have thirty roubles, only ten of which are openly known to be mine.

So, we can now count on our fingers the days left till our fate is decided. In the event of our not being allowed to fly, we will go on foot. There are about 100 kilometres to go, but we will get there somehow. Mother's dream nowadays is to break away from noisy city life and settle down in some provincial village, where there would be a secondary school for me, we could set up house in a country cottage, I could turn my attention to agricultural studies, and we could live out our lives in tranquillity and comfort, like Tina. Mother is weary of her life. She is attracted, for example, by the sort of life that Tina was leading in Schlüsselburg: a peaceful, calm life, without any scrapes or stormy incidents. But perhaps I am mistaken and this is only a passing fancy of Mother's. However, I do remember that she has had such dreams before, of life in a rural environment, but this is a life that has demands of its own... Well, right now there are plenty of other things to cope with. Outside the window the anti-aircraft guns are in action, shells are exploding – it's not the moment for me to be dealing with such thoughts.

Today, incidentally, Mother told me that the level of starvation we are enduring now is worse than that experienced in 1918. In 1918, according to Mother, the so-called 'travelling with sacks' was a very highly-developed form of black marketeering. People would travel to remote villages, get bread, flour and butter there, return to Petrograd (as Leningrad was then called) and sell all these goods straight out of their sacks – for astronomical prices, it goes without saying. But those who had money at the time were well fed, whereas nowadays a man could have millions to spend but, if he lost his monthly food and bread ration cards, he would inevitably die of starvation, unless he were some kind of exceptionally enterprising person.

The situation on the front lines is better. The German troops are retreating in disorder towards Taganrog. We are on their heels.

So, this is the beginning of the rout of Germany – around Moscow, around Rostov and around Leningrad. Let the Nazi swine be butchered with all speed, damn them! But when they have been slaughtered, they will give off such a rotten stench that no one in their vicinity will remain alive.

Tomorrow I must go to school. Without fail. If the evacuation business comes to anything, they will only let me out of the city on condition that I have been a registered student. Which is why it is essential for me to attend school.

How I would love to eat some bread now! Bread! Bread!

1 December 1941. The beginning of a new month. The beginning of a new ten-day ration period. I am writing this in the morning. I got to school at eight this morning. I was told that, starting today, lessons will begin at ten and students will be allowed inside the school building from twenty to ten. I set off for home. I stopped in at the company canteen and had a hot tea with a chocolate sweet there. For the sweet they clipped a coupon for ten grams of confectionery. I came home. At half-past nine I was intending to go back to school, but the air-raid warning went. Now, as I write this, the alert is still in force. It must surely be gone ten by now.

These days I hoard my energy so carefully that even the decision to walk along the corridor to the dining room seems an important one to me. My whole body feels weakened. My legs are leaden, my knees are weak, it is a struggle to get up out of a chair, there is weakness throughout my body. And there will probably be nothing to eat until six or seven this evening. At home Mother has hidden the butter. I searched around for it, but I couldn't find it, and I can't eat raw horsemeat. If the alert goes on for another two hours or so, I won't go to school. Where would be the sense? But I ought to go just the same. I will take only some of the textbooks with me.

This means that the Germans will be starting their air-raids now from ten in the morning or, rather, from half-past nine. And I should be setting off for school at precisely that time. What am I to do?

Anyway, I want to sum up what the month of November has taught me and how 30 November differs from 30 October. First of all, lessons began at school in October, which destroyed all my striving for knowledge because of the atmosphere in which they were conducted. And so I finished with school, or so it seemed. I switched to the daily grind of standing in queues. At once all my idealistic views were replaced by strictly material concerns. The main requirement of life during the month has remained the same – food.

It must be said that the food situation on 30 October was worse for us than on 30 November. But at the same time, needless to say, our food requirements remained unchanged. 'If there is anything edible going – put it in your mouth.' In this slogan there will soon be a case for adding the prefix 'in' to the word 'edible'. Hopes have stayed the same, but it would be true to say that their practical basis has to some extent been strengthened now. If evacuation seemed a somewhat abstract concept to me on 30 October, it is now a question of the coming week.

What can be said about the past month, however, is that this month, a month of suffering and tears, of family squabbles and constant hunger, has robbed me of half the strength that I had before. I never had enough to eat, not once in the whole month. No day passed without us being bombed or shelled. On top of the

114

hunger, there was not a single day that was not also darkened by fear for my own life and for the lives of Mother and Ira.

But there were two positive events that occurred in November. Our relationship with Anfissa Nikolaievna changed for the better. Thinking that she will be evacuated in a matter of days, she has been letting us have a fair amount of food and, given the current situation, without charging us or asking for anything in exchange. The second positive event was Tina's evacuation to Siberia from Boksitogorsk. Her last letter, which we received a few days ago, said that she was on a train and passing through the town of Bui, which is situated in the Yaroslavskaya region.

All my hopes now seem to be balanced on a knife-edge, maintaining a fairly uneasy equilibrium. What will the response be to Mother's application to be flown out? In any case, we should prepare ourselves for an evacuation on foot. Although there are rumours circulating about such an evacuation, it is going on at the moment in a spontaneous and disorganized manner. There are many rumours about this evacuation. There is talk of feeding points being set up along the way, of transporting children by lorry, and so on. But people are capable of inventing any old thing!

14

Saving the Children

Lidiya Okhapkina continues her story:

There were hungry rats running about in the apartment, squeaking.
They would nibble at the wallpaper, which in those days was stuck
on with a wallpaper paste made of flour and water. The room I had
was unfurnished. There were just two narrow iron bedsteads in it,
on one of which Tolya slept, on the other my daughter and me.
There was also a kitchen table, which the old lady had allowed me
to take from the kitchen. All our own furniture had been left
behind in Volkhov Village. Rosa, a seventeen year old girl, and her
aunt lived in the apartment. This old lady's husband was a
professor, and he had been evacuated along with the institute where
he worked, but she had refused to go because she was afraid to leave
her belongings. Their room was lavishly furnished: carpets, a piano
and good furniture. Later, in January 1942, she died of starvation.
She came to me a number of times complaining about Rosa, saying
that she hardly gave her any bread. It was Rosa who went to fetch
the bread, the aunt herself was afraid to go out into the street. I felt
sorry for her, but what could I do? I had troubles enough of my
own. It was a long time since I had received any letters from my
husband, and I didn't know where he was or what was happening to
him. And he didn't know our new address on Vasilievsky Island
either. I couldn't help thinking that we might never see one another
again. But I thought about it somehow without any particularly
intense pain, because it seemed to me that it didn't matter too

much – we would all soon be dead of starvation anyway.

In my thoughts I hoped that death would come for me and my children at the same time, because I was afraid that, if I were killed in the street, for example, the children would be crying frantically and calling: 'Mama! Mama!' and then they would die of starvation in the icy room. My Ninochka cried all the time, with long-drawn-out wails that prevented her from falling asleep. This crying, like moaning, was driving me crazy. Then, in an attempt to get her to sleep, I gave her my blood to suck. There had been no milk in my breasts for a long time, and the breasts themselves had completely vanished, gone. So I pricked my arm above the elbow with a needle and applied my daughter's mouth to the place. She sucked gently and then fell asleep. But it was ages before I could get off to sleep myself. I would start counting, then lose my place. I remembered how when I read Tolstoy's *War and Peace*, Pierre Besukhov would also count up to 1,000, to put himself to sleep. But I would lose count. I could never stop thinking about where I could get some food, at least something. I had visions all the time of loaves of bread, or of me gathering potatoes in a field. I would collect a whole sackful, and it would be too heavy for me to carry away. I did once manage to buy some carpenter's glue from someone in a marketplace. In those days people used to make a jelly from it. So I made some too, and I ate it. I gave some to little Tolya, but I was afraid to give it to Ninochka. But then we started getting constipated from eating the glue, so I stopped making it. On another occasion I managed to buy some pork skin. It was more tasty, but it had to be boiled for a long time to get it to soften, and I was having to economize on paraffin since I had so little of it left.

It was dreadfully cold in the apartment. There was hoar frost on the walls, like you see inside barns in the winter. When I had to change Ninochka's nappy, I would slide my hand under the blanket to put a dry one on her, so that she wouldn't catch cold, and I would throw the wet nappy out onto the floor, where it would soon freeze, the way wet washing freezes on a line outdoors. I didn't have a thermometer, but the air temperature was certainly below zero. By then I had lost so much weight that there was no flesh on my legs

117

at all. My chest was like a man's – just nipples. On my face the skin was stretched tightly over my cheek-bones, my eyes were deep-sunken. The children were also very skinny, and my heart would falter when I saw their bony little arms and legs and their trans-parent little faces and huge eyes. There was no firewood at all. There was nothing to heat water with or cook anything. Rosa told me that they had a little coal left in the basement, but that it was a terrible place to go to, because they had been piling the dead bodies there. I said that didn't matter – we had to go there just the same. We took buckets and went. There were indeed a number of corpses lying there. We tried not to look at them. We loaded the coal as quickly as we could, using our bare hands, and left in haste. There was no electric light either, and we had lit oil lamps. I had a wick made from cotton-wool in a little glass jar with some machine oil in it, which I had bartered something for. It gave off a dim light and it was dark in our room. Big shadows formed on the walls and the smoke trailed upwards in a slender thread. There was no running water in the cistern either, and I had to go to the Neva to get it. I would walk there pulling a child's sled with a bucket and a pan on it. We needed a lot of water because, apart from any cooking, the nappies had to be washed as well…

I had become absolutely indifferent to the air-raid warnings, which were fairly rare, but the shelling in the streets happened more often. Once I went out for bread while the shelling was going on, because the queues were shorter at such times, and I came under heavy shellfire. I had intended to run to the entrance of a nearby building, but, as it happened, I was caught going along beside a long fence. The shells were flying and exploding very near to me. Someone shouted at me from the other side of the street: 'You fool! Get down at once! Get down!' I dropped down and pressed myself to the wall. Then I looked around, stood up, then dropped down again with my face right in the snow. I lay there for several seconds, my heart pounding. I began to crawl forward. Basically, I was advancing like a frontline soldier.

The winter of 1941-42 was exceptionally cold. The temperature fell to thirty or forty degrees below zero. All the time I kept wondering where I could get hold of some firewood. When I was leaving Volkhov Village, I had filled the wardrobe with chopped firewood and had hidden a gramophone underneath it. I was keen to go there but the thing was, there was no public transport – the tramway wasn't operating at that time – and I would have had to walk there and back, a really long distance. I kept putting it off, but one day I got ready to go. I fed the children, locked them in, and set off early in the morning. Can you imagine the journey from Vasilievsky Island to Volkhov Village? I crossed the frozen Neva by a well-trodden path, entered Liteiny Prospect and kept staring around at the buildings, which stood in grim rows. Many had broken windows, which showed up dark, like empty eye-sockets. Others had a corner or a part of the building sliced off by a shell. And people were still living in the other part. I crossed paths with other pedestrians. They were all walking slowly, barely moving their legs. All muffled up, with thin grey faces; even some men with headscarves tied on over their hats.

Yes, the city was wounded, like a man who has been in combat. But it was alive and, even though it was living a hard life, it was not dying; people still had some hope, their determination had not deserted them. This nightmare, this horror, would surely have to end sometime. When I reached the Nevsky, my heart was constricted with emotion: it was almost deserted, piled high with snow. Many buildings were half destroyed, their windows boarded over with plywood. Trams and trolley-buses stood there, also covered with snow. The Gostiny Dvor had been scorched by fire. The stallions had gone from the Anichkov Bridge.

A five-storey building used to stand at the corner of Ligovka and Rasieszhaya Streets. It was burning, but it was a strange kind of fire. On each storey the window-frames and floors were alight, flames were crawling slowly out of the windows, seeming to lick the window-frames and sills, moving unhurriedly. There was no wind, and a little blue flame was creeping steadily around the building. They were saying that this building had been set on fire by people using little home-made stoves and that it had already been burning for three days. There was a great deal of assorted furniture

119

scattered around the building – beds, broken wardrobes, chests, etc. By then there was no one to remove such junk and no one was keeping an eye on it.

When I eventually reached our old home, I saw that the topmost floor of the building had virtually been demolished. The roof had burned while I was still living there. There were still some families living on the ground floor, which is where I used to live as well. Maria Nikolaievna and her grown-up daughter used to be my next-door neighbours. They had both become extremely thin, but they still looked better than people living in the centre of the city. I said to Maria Nikolaievna: 'How are you getting on? I see you didn't leave, then?' And she replied: 'Where would I go? It's not so bad here now. I managed to dig a few potatoes the other side of the railway line. And there's masses of firewood. You can break off planks and logs from the half-burnt wooden houses, and use them to stoke the stove and cook. And the bombing raids have almost stopped.'

I said: 'Well, where I am, I have no firewood at all.'

'So take a ride out here, then,' she said.

And I: 'What could I take a ride on? There is no public transport at all, you know. I came here on foot.'

And, having reminded myself of this, I said goodbye to her and entered my old room. The windows – there were two of them – someone had boarded up with planks. Snow had forced its way through the crevices between the planks. Snow lay everywhere: on the table, on the bed, on the sofa and on the floor. My heart sank at the sight of my things, and the memory of our peaceful life flooded over me painfully. But there was no time to sit and sigh, and I started to get a move on. I took the gramophone, which I wanted to barter for bread later on, and gathered up a few toys from the floor for little Tolya. I remember that I took a little clockwork elephant and a teddy bear for him, and a celluloid parrot for my daughter. I bundled everything together and put it on the sled, along with a small amount of firewood. I also scraped some congealed fat from the side of the kitchen table, where we used to hang our frying-pan and the fat would drip down, and I ate it

120

straight away. I thought about that little blob of fat more than once, on nights when I so much wanted something to eat and to get some sleep. How I managed to get back, I can't remember. I used up my last remaining strength. On the way home I bought our bread ration and ate almost all of it. By then I was no longer gawping about, but was dragging the sled like a knackered horse, thinking of nothing but the fact that the children were waiting for me. By the time I arrived home, it was completely dark.

I constantly went about in my husband's felt boots and wore two overcoats: my own and my husband's on top of it. Everyone else was bundled up like that too. Some people would throw old people's shawls over their shoulders on top of their overcoats, and even quilted blankets.

Whenever I went out, my daughter would invariably start to cry. To stop her crying, I used to give her a little piece of dried rye bread, and she would suck at it for a long time. And I had given it to her on this occasion too. But, by the time I was locking the door, I could hear that she had begun to cry. What it was, little Tolya had taken the bread from her, because I hadn't given him any; there wasn't any more left. I went back in and I smacked him for the first time. He sobbed loudly, and I felt terribly sorry for him as well. I told him that, if he kept on taking things from Ninochka, I would throw him out into the street. He said: 'Don't do it, Mama, I won't do it again.' I kissed him, wrapped him in a blanket, and left. That day we could redeem our rations, as they used to say then, and I got 200 grams of millet on my ration card. I had surrendered the children's ration cards – I had enrolled them in a children's dining hall – and this went a long way towards keeping us afloat. I received food for both children there. Breakfast in the mornings: very watery porridge, certainly, and in stingy little helpings. And for dinner some kind of soup and something for the main course: mashed potatoes or porridge again. If we had not had this – the meals in the dining hall – we would have faced even worse starvation. My son would sit and watch the alarm clock all the time. I had explained to him that when the big hand was on twelve and the little hand on ten, we would go for breakfast; and when the big hand was on twelve again and the little one on three, it would be time for our dinner. So he constantly watched the clock. I divided the millet that I had got on my card roughly into two and I cooked a thin porridge for supper twice. On one occasion when I got back home after going out for bread, I found little Tolya sitting on the floor and poking at something there with a matchstick. I asked him what he was doing. He told me that he was digging out grains of millet from the cracks between the floorboards. I had spilled a few when I was cooking the porridge in the dark, and now he was digging them out and eating them along with the dirt.

I thought: 'My God, how hungry he must be, but what can I do, what can I feed him on?' He was so thin that he rarely got out of bed any more, and he would say to me over and over again:

'Mama! I could eat a whole pail of porridge and a whole sack of potatoes.'

I would attempt to distract him. I would try to tell him fairy stories, but he would barely listen and would keep interrupting me:

'You know, Mama, I could eat a loaf of bread as big as that!' and he would point to the round washtub.

I would say: 'No, you couldn't, you wouldn't have enough room in your tummy.'

And he would protest: 'I could eat it, Mama, I could! I wouldn't sleep, I would just eat and eat all the time!'

He looked like a little jackdaw, all mouth and big brown eyes, and they were so sad. And his little legs were so thin, just the knee-caps jutting right out. It was a long time since his hair had been cut, it had grown long and was always untidy. On one occasion they gave me 200 grams of dried peas on my card. I decided to make a thin soup out of them. I prepared it in the oven and wrapped it in a blanket, so that the steam would soften it up more. Then I called in on my neighbour. She was dying. I stayed there for a while and then left. When I got back I saw that the saucepan had been unwrapped. I said to Tolya: 'You've been at it already.'

He said: 'I only had one little spoonful, Mama, just one, to try it.'

I said: 'All right, let's eat it, then.' I ladled it out with a spoon and a piece of rag came up with it, which had been used to bandage his hands. His impetigo had almost gone, and the scabs had already fallen off, but I still kept him bandaged, so that he wouldn't infect me or Ninochka, and the rag had fallen off. What should I do?

He immediately began to whimper: 'I didn't do it on purpose, Mama, it fell off by itself.'

What was I to do? It would have been such a shame to tip the soup away. So we ate it. To this day I have been unable to forget this incident, and Tolya remembered it for a long time afterwards too...

Shortly after I had brought the gramophone home I pinned an advert up near the bread shop, saying that I had a gramophone to barter in exchange for bread. The next day a military man turned up, bringing a whole loaf of bread. I asked him if he could give just a little more. He replied: 'I would do so with pleasure but, unfortunately, this is all that I have.' I threw in the few records that I had as well. Soon afterwards I pinned up an advert to say that I had a manual sewing-machine to sell. I had brought it with me back when we were moved in September. Before long a woman came and offered me slightly more than half a loaf, not a whole one. I was very reluctant to part with the machine, but I had no choice, I let it go. The woman didn't look particularly worn down. I asked her where she worked. She told me to mind my own business. Bread had such a high value. But I was never able to barter clothes for bread. Nobody wanted them. I had nothing else left to barter.

At the end of December 1941, I met a young woman when we were standing in the bread queue. She had called me from the queue and asked me to buy her bread ration for her, because she was standing a long way back and I was nearer. She had three ration cards too – two children's ones and a dependant's one – the same as I had. It all had to be taken together as a single purchase, because they wouldn't weigh out two separate lots for one person. I agreed, bought the bread, and we divided it in two. Then we got into conversation. She also lived on Vasilievsky Island a few streets away from me and her husband was also away at the Front. She said that she still had some firewood (whereas I no longer had any at all), and invited us to move to her place. I agreed and that same day

I dragged the children and some necessary belongings over there. She was a very impatient person and, once she had got her bread, she ate it up straight away. I, on the other hand, divided ours into three pieces, so that it could be eaten in the morning, the afternoon and the evening. We would go to the dining hall for dinner together and take it in turns to fetch the bread. She would go one day, I the next. One evening when I looked, I realized that my bread was missing. I used to put our bread into a little briefcase and hang it high above the sofa on which all three of us slept. It was beyond Tolya's reach. I used to hang it up there because the rats could find it anywhere else and eat it. I asked her why she had taken my bread. She denied that she had.

Not long afterwards, one of her children – the little girl – died. Towards the end of January, the 27th – I still remember the date – Zhenia, as she was called, went to fetch the bread, while I stayed behind with the children and was boiling water on the little iron stove that we had bartered bread for. About two hours later she came in and said that she had lost my ration cards. I went white with distress and asked her how we were going to divide up the bread in the circumstances. And she then said that this was not going to happen. She said I would have to excuse her, but she had no intention of dying for my benefit. As it happened, I still had one child's ration card left, because we used to buy bread in advance, but I had kept one card back to use on 31 January. I said: 'At least give me one card. It would be absolutely unfair if the two of you were living off three cards, while the three of us were living off one.' She refused. Then I said that I was going to leave her. 'Well, you are free to go!' she said. And so there I was, once more dragging the children and our things back to our cold little room, narrow as a coffin. There was no one in the apartment. Rosa had also gone off somewhere, when we left to move in with that woman. It was unbearably cold in our room. Hoar frost on the walls, snow on the windowsill. 'My God,' I thought, 'how can we survive in such cold, with almost no bread for the coming five days?' I entered the room belonging to the professor's late wife, took two of her chairs,

124

broke them up and lit the stove. Then I ran down to the basement and scraped up a little more coal. I ran over to the dining hall to fetch the dinner. That night I couldn't get to sleep. I was haunted by bleak thoughts about dying. I nearly went off my head because of these thoughts and my distress. Five days without bread! When it wouldn't even have been enough anyway! I got out of bed and threw myself to my knees and began to pray, praying and weeping. There was no icon and, besides, I didn't know a single prayer. My children had never been baptized and I didn't really believe in God myself. To tell the truth, when there was an air-raid alert on, I sometimes whispered in my thoughts: 'Lord, save us, don't let us die.' But this time I was putting a different request to God, using other words. 'Lord,' I whispered fervently, 'You can see how I am suffering, how hungry I am and how hungry my little children are. I am at the end of my tether. Lord, I beg, send us death, but make it so that we all die together. I can't go on living any longer. You can see how tormented I am, Lord, take pity on these blameless children' – and other such words.

The next day someone started knocking on the front door. I hadn't gone out for bread and so was at home. I ran and asked who it was. A man's voice asked if this was where Lidiya Georgievna Okhapkina lived. I let him in. He was a messenger from the Front, from my husband. He handed me a small parcel and a letter. Vasili had written: 'Darling Lidiya...' Having read no more than that, I burst into tears and I said to myself: 'If only he could see what has become of his Lidiya!' Further on in the letter he wrote that he was sending a kilo of semolina, a kilo of rice and two packets of biscuits. For some reason I read this out loud. After the word 'rice', Tolya piped up piteously: 'Mama, make some porridge, but make it a bit thicker.' Those were his exact words. The officer, who was a lieutenant, suddenly began to blow his nose loudly and to wipe away the tears that had appeared on his cheeks when he looked at all of us. He said: 'It is awful when children are so starving hungry. We will get you out. Be patient just a little bit longer. I will tell your husband about you. And the Nazis, they will pay for it all. For all your tears, for the fact that you are starving like this, for everything.'

For just that one time I made a thicker porridge, as Tolya had asked, and then I began economizing again. But no matter how much I tried to eke it out, we had soon eaten it all. And, on top of that, once more there was no firewood and we simply froze. I was wearing an overcoat and felt boots indoors. The children were dressed in their winter coats too and were wrapped in quilted blankets.

Rosa turned up once and said that they were distributing vouchers for firewood at the District Executive Committee. And first priority was to be given to those who had children.

I went there immediately and I was given a voucher for one cubic metre of firewood. The next day I borrowed a sled from the caretaker and Rosa and I set off. The firewood was somewhere beyond Smolenskoye Cemetery.

With great difficulty, one log at a time, we dragged the wood into the kitchen. The logs were one metre long. We immediately lit the stove. It had to be fed from the corridor, and it fronted into both our room and Rosa's. Rosa also gave me several books from the professor's library to get the fire going. For the first time it was really warm in our place. I was extremely tired and wanted to sleep. I had pushed the damper in a bit too soon and opened the air-vent into our room. We all got badly gassed. I woke up because my daughter had started to cry. My head was splitting. I stood up, swaying about, then fell down again. But somehow, in falling, I pushed the door open. Cool air began to flow in from the corridor. I lay there unconscious for I don't remember how many minutes. Then it was as though someone had nudged me.

The children – how were they? Unsteady on my feet, I grabbed my daughter. She was silent and hardly breathing. I carried her out to the kitchen, then I picked up little Tolya and, using my last reserves of strength, dragged him over and sat down beside them myself. We all almost died from the fumes. Tolya remained unconscious for a long time.

We started to starve again. By then February 1942 was nearing its end. We had eaten what was in the parcel a long time ago. More than once Tolya suggested to me: 'Mama, let's make fumes again and die. Our heads will ache at first, but then we will fall asleep.' It is unbearable to hear this coming from a child.

15

The Noose Tightens

Yura's diary continues:

2 December 1941. In the evenings Mother and Ira lay on a sort of torture for me. At table Ira eats deliberately slowly, not just to derive pleasure from eating, but also to enjoy the feeling that she is still eating while the rest of us, who have already finished eating, sit there watching her with hungry eyes. Mother is always the first to eat up her share, and then she takes a little bit from each of us. When the bread is being divided up, Ira bursts into tears if my little piece outweighs hers by so much as half a gram. Ira is always at Mother's side. I normally spend time with Mother only in the evening, though we see one another briefly in the morning. It is probably because of this that Ira is always in Mother's good books. It seems that I am an egoist, as even Mother has told me. But I can remember how I used to be friends with Vovka Shmailov and how at that time I made no distinction between what was his and what was mine, and how Mother – in this instance Mother herself – was then the egoistical one. She wouldn't give Vovka books that I had two copies of, and so on. So why has she wanted to form my character in that direction since then? And it is still not too late to undo it now.

In the old days, to feel properly satisfied all day long, I would have had to eat two or three canteen meals during the day, plus a decent supper and breakfast on top of that, and various snacks. Nowadays I have to be satisfied with 100 grams of biscuits in the morning, nothing at all during the day, and a bowl of soup or thin broth in the evening. Apart from that, water. Water in the guises of tea, coffee, soup – just water. That is my menu.

As for being evacuated, once again everything has gone up in smoke. Or almost everything. Mother has now become afraid to go. She says: 'We would end up in some godforsaken place...' And so on, and so forth.

3 December 1941. Mother has fallen ill. She didn't even go to work today. High temperature, aching joints, heavy swollen legs. Is it water retention? And it is so hard... I can't write any more. I'm in such a down-hearted mood. I am sitting in the kitchen, the wood is crackling in the stove, and my sick mother is stretched out on the chest by my side. Dear God!

According to the news bulletin, Tikhvin has been taken by the Germans. Sevastopol continues to resist.

Mother is ill, Ira is just a child, there's been nothing from Tina – we don't even know her address – and I am exhausted, worn down, scarcely able to stand on my own two feet. Whatever will happen next?

4 December 1941. Busy all day. I got up early, did the rounds of the bread shops, got some sweet biscuits, then I went to the medical centre in Pravda Street. I wanted to summon a doctor for Mother, but it turned out to be the wrong one for our address. I had to go on to a different medical centre in Matyanin Lane. Then another queue, chopping firewood, more miseries.

Mother has been suspended from her job at the Trades Union Regional Committee because she is on the evacuation list. She is lying here ill. The doctor who came to see her diagnosed 'flu and cardiac insufficiency, which caused the swollen legs, pains in her sides, etc. The remedy – adequate food. But there isn't any. So Mother has taken to her bed. She is really unwell and, in any case, she has no job to go to. It is possible that the evacuation will be on foot, but Mother with her swollen legs and her illness, Ira with her lack of strength, and me with all my other worries about them and

129

about myself, people with sixty kilos of luggage, if not more – we would never be able to undertake a lengthy, snowy journey of some 300 kilometres, spending a month en route... And so this is how our whole life will end: frost-bitten along the way and left behind ill in some remote hospital, or exhausted by daily starvation, swollen, barely dragging out our miserable existence...

That is really all that I can say today or, rather, all that I have been able to write. I remain indifferent to news of the Front, whether they are winning or not, and untouched by any political event. What is going on around us, here in the apartment? The various neighbours are flying out over the next few days. But Mother is ill, she needs good food that can't be found anywhere, she needs tranquillity. And I am exhausted, drained. Ira is worn down too. What are we to do?

5 December 1941. Mother is right: we should always believe that things will get better. For the time being we must believe that we will be evacuated. So it should be. And it will be. Even though Mother can hardly walk – she will recover; even though Ira complains of pains in her left side – they will pass. Even though neither Mother nor I have the proper footwear – we have neither felt boots nor warm clothes – we will break out of this prison of starvation that Leningrad has become. By now it is evening, there is an alert on, the anti-aircraft guns are firing, bombs are exploding. The most awful lottery is being played out, in which winning means life for a person and losing means death. But that's how life is.

Anfissa Nikolaievna and her family are not leaving tomorrow. They will leave in a day or two. Lucky people!

Hunger. The cruellest hunger!

Gradually, little by little, an image of Anfissa Nikolaievna is taking shape before me. From her quarrels with her husband, in the course of which they both reveal something of their lives, from conversations with them, and now from the sad and deeply heartfelt story told by her husband, the image I have of her is to some extent emerging from the shadows.

130

Anfissa Nikolaievna is twenty-seven years old. When she was fourteen, she was already in love or, rather, she was the mistress of some rough type who, by brute force, got her addicted to alcohol. Since then she has never been able to break free from wine, vodka, etc. She used to suffer from attacks of *delirium tremens*, get falling-down drunk in the street. But, when sober, she was stunningly beautiful and captivating. This was evidently how she was when her present husband met her. He dumped his former wife and his daughter for her, after receiving a letter from her in which, in the throes of some urge towards rehabilitation, she begged him 'to get her out of this filthy pit' by marrying her. And so a new life began for her. The husband earns 2,000 roubles a month, the wife spends forty roubles a day. Travelling to different health resorts, no attempt to wean his wife off the bottle neglected, quarrels over money... The husband is himself a slightly unbalanced man, at one time he was even in some psychiatric hospital. And his wife often left him completely penniless before payday, drinking the money away. But at the same time Anfissa is undoubtedly a person who, when sober, has an amazingly nice nature. It might well be, of course, that this is nothing more than a show, but just the same... In any event, Anfissa Nikolaievna is a person whose nature is extremely difficult to fathom.

6 December 1941. Eleven in the morning. Anfissa Nikolaievna and her husband have not left. Their departure has been postponed for two or three days. Mother and Ira have gone off to the Regional Committee. Mother now needs to sort out a number of things. The exit permit, whether to fly out or join the neighbours' group, warm clothes for Mother and felt boots for me, getting a lock put on the door. But Mother still has very little energy. For energy you need food. Food first and foremost. It is the only source of physical energy.

Mother has chosen the final destination for the evacuation. It is to be Barnaul and its surrounding area. In general, the whole business boils down to two things: the method of travel and the clothes to wear. The response from Smolny has evidently not come yet. This is bad. It would be nice if we could be included in the neighbours' group.

Mother is faced with two more difficulties. The first is to secure our financial position by making an application to the Regional Committee and by selling off a few things, and the second is to arrange to finalize her release from work, which is a great deal simpler.

But there is another major issue, and that is food. Without it we are not going to be able to make our legs work.

Yesterday Anfissa Nikolaievna gave us about 300 grams of dried peas, thinking that she would be leaving today. If only she could have given us 800 or 900 grams!

I am still facing some very daunting difficulties: rid myself of lice, go to the public baths, get a haircut, sort my books out, find some firewood, buy some food, settle things at school. I feel that there is not very long to go before the day when I overtax my strength and take to my bed. But if I do take to my bed, it won't be for five minutes!

I didn't read the newspapers yesterday, I know nothing, I am not keeping track of current events. As for our Leningrad Front, the situation is bad, which is one thing that even I am well aware of. Yesterday I heard in some queue that they had actually put a stop to the evacuation on foot that had been taking place over the Lake Ladoga ice. People had been given white camouflage overalls and with them on they had walked eighty kilometres through snowstorms, over the ice, without any stops and without food. Many of them couldn't stand up to it and died.

It goes without saying that we can't expect any help from Tina now. She has better things to spend her salary on nowadays. The luckiest member of our family. In her last letter from Kirov, she wrote that her situation was satisfactory. And two or three months ago, in a letter from Boksitogorsk, she complained of a shortage of sweet things. Which means that nowadays she has the food situation well in hand. She has before her a choice of all kinds of delicacies, she doesn't so much as give a thought to bread. But does she even think about us? Does she? And in what way? Does she know about the famine in Leningrad, about the bombing raids, the shelling? Or perhaps she has given herself over to gluttony these days? Anything is possible. I am so starving hungry that I can't bring myself to share a crumb of bread with my mother. Since this morning this has been such a heavy weight on my heart, so utterly painful, and I know that this is how it will be in the future, if I don't stop myself now. But how do I make myself stop? Painful, painful.

7 December 1941. Yesterday several interesting events occurred. Having arranged it with Gromov, Mother took illegal possession of the office-worker's ration card belonging to Sukharev, who had been crossed off the Regional Committee's list of active workers. Using this card, we bought 200 grams of macaroni, 350 grams of sweets, and 125 grams of bread yesterday. And, with the exception of the macaroni, we ate the whole lot yesterday too. Mother was also given a chit addressed to the chairman of the District Executive Committee for her to be issued some oilcake. But I'm sure nothing will come of it. One of Mother's friends promised to have some old felt boots ready to give to her today, but I couldn't go and fetch them this morning – it was so bitterly cold.

These next ten days will be decisive for our fate. The most important issues that must be solved are: what to wear on the journey and which people to travel with. Oh, if only I could eat my fill at least twice in a row! Otherwise, where am I going to find the energy and the strength to confront all the difficulties that lie ahead of us? Mother is ill again. Today she got only three hours' sleep, from three till six in the morning. It is absolutely essential for me to go and fetch the warm clothes we were promised. But it is so freezing cold outdoors and my body is so weary that I am afraid even to venture outside.

I began to keep a diary at the beginning of summer and now it is already winter. Could I possibly have imagined that my diary would turn out to be something like this?

I am beginning to set some money aside. By now I have fifty-six roubles in cash, whose existence is known to me alone. The stove has gone out and the cold is gradually gaining the upper hand in the kitchen. I must put my overcoat on, so as not to freeze to the bone. And here's me wanting to go to Siberia! But my feeling is that, if I were given some food, I would shake off all this melancholy, all this despondency, the weariness would fly away, my tongue would be set free and I would become a human being again, not just the pale shadow of one.

Igor, Anfissa Nikolaievna's brother, comes to visit us every evening. Anfissa Nikolaievna feeds him as though she were fattening him up for Christmas: she has given him all her reserves of dried bread. Now, if she does go off somewhere, there will be absolutely nothing left for us. Perhaps she will still leave behind for us her pass to the tuberculosis clinic near the Klinsky marketplace, which would allow us to get half a litre of milk a day in her place. It is an area which comes under shellfire every day, so that it is not just a long way to go, you put your life in danger too.

By now I have lost about ten or fifteen kilos, not more. Perhaps even less, but, if so, only on account of my excessive consumption of water. In the old days a glass and a half of tea was enough for me in the morning, but nowadays six are not sufficient.

8 December 1941. Today was the day I lost Sukharev's ration card for butter, valid for the first ten-day period; the very one that Mother obtained illegally. So what am I going to do now? I am afraid, mortally afraid, that this whole story of the misappropriation of Sukharev's cards will surface and, if it did, my life would be ruined, as well as Mother's and Ira's. I lost it – I know for certain – in the company canteen. I most likely left the counter assistant holding it. If only the matter would end there… if only! I don't know whether I should broach the topic with Mother or not. If Mother is in a good mood – which is unlikely – then I will, but if not, I'll keep my mouth shut about the loss.

I'm in anguish, terrible anguish, about this card! I can't even think about anything else.

Another possible scenario: the card turns out to have been lost at home and Anfissa Nikolaievna finds it. A simple question occurs to her: how could this card have come into our hands and nobody else's? She examines the stamp – the Regional Committee's – and, until recently, this stamp was in Mother's keeping. She reports all this to her husband, who finds out who Sukharev is – and Mother is taken before a tribunal, then comes expulsion from the Party, the firing-squad, etc.

It is three in the afternoon now, and Mother left for work at nine o'clock this morning. What could she be doing? Is it possible that nothing will happen today to advance our evacuation by a single step? To leave, leave, leave! The fundamental issue. Warm clothes. You wouldn't get far without warm clothes.

9 December 1941. It turned out that Mother had the card after all. Yesterday I used it to buy 200 grams of sour cream. We ate it yesterday too. Today we also ate 100 grams of yesterday's fat ration, but we still have 15 grams left, thank God.

Yesterday Mother obtained two quilted jackets and some warm trousers and brought them home. Now it's the turn of the felt boots.

The question of the flight out has not been settled. But I am hoping that we will fly. It is true that Anfissa and her husband were refused permission to fly out, but Katsura and his wife have been given permission to fly as far as Vologda. In any case, it is a very dodgy business. At one time there were quite regular departures, but now, so Anfissa's husband told me, they have petered out. The lists of potential evacuees are being severely pruned, while the number of those wishing to be evacuated includes almost everyone – whoever you mention it to – so the issue is becoming more serious than it was before. According to Anfissa's husband, they were evacuating people in three-ton lorries earlier on, but now they are using only thirty-hundredweight ones.

The Regional Committee has provided Mother with some money for the evacuation. Yesterday we counted our money: we have over 1,300 roubles. Mother will be without a job after 10 December. I think that if a positive reply came from Smolny, I would be as happy as I have ever been. This reply must come, it is obliged to come, it will come – how could it fail to come?

It would be nice if we could fly out on the twelfth. We could buy our ration of sweets for the new ten-day period on the eleventh and fly out sucking them. If that happened, I believe that even my memories of this awful starvation would begin to let up a bit. After all, what actually happened to me? I ate a cat, I stole spoonfuls of food from Anfissa Nikolaievna's pans, I filched an extra crumb from Mother and Ira, sometimes I cheated them, I got frozen stiff in endless queues, I cursed and fought in shop doorways for the right to enter and buy 100 grams of butter. I became encrusted with filth, I was crawling with lice, I got too exhausted to find the energy to get up out of my chair – it was such a huge effort for me! Non-stop bombing and shelling, standing fire-watch duty in the attics at school, squabbles and scenes at home over sharing out the food. I came to recognize the value of crumbs of bread, which I gathered up from the table with my fingers, and I came to understand, although perhaps not quite entirely, my coarse and egoistical character. 'Death is the only remedy for a hunchback' – so the saying goes. I wonder if it might be the remedy for my character?

How many clean pages are still left in my diary? I count thirty-six and there were 200 to begin with. In about a fortnight's time, this diary will be six months old, six months of war. I have written about many things in this diary. At first my notes were of a descriptive nature, then they took a philosophical turn. Each day that I live through provides a page, or even two. And how often a day's notes begin with a description of hunger; of hunger and cold! Now, when I see before me the prospect of evacuation, I somehow manage to suppress such thoughts. But what if this hope disappears? What then? How will I go on living?

And now it is either shelling again or an air-raid alert. You can hear some firing going on somewhere. Mother has gone to work. She's out there, under the shellfire. She has to put the seal on the Regional Committee's reserves. Will our hope of flying out be realized today? Or not?

It is time to stop. I have already covered a whole page with my philosophical scribbling, without any real reason. To get back to reality: what are we going to eat today? It would be good if they

136

would let us use our coupons for the second ten-day period in the canteen today. If not, we will be left with nothing to eat all day. A whole day. Twenty-four long hours.

At the beginning of December, the 'Road of Life' had yet to become a real life-saver for the Leningraders. It was no more than a track across the ice, and the ice itself was precarious: it wore thin, it broke; it was not possible to load the lorries properly. German aircraft were bombing the road, there were constant dogfights going on overhead as Soviet air-defence squadrons struggled to beat off the attacks, in spite of the shortage of fighter planes.

Lorries crossing the Ladoga ice would fall into the bomb craters and sink beneath the water. Getting goods to Lake Ladoga had also become a problem, since the road to Tikhvin had been cut, and the goods had to be transported by lorry over almost impassable tracks. As a result, the city had so far received negligibly little over the ice road. But detachments of the Fifty-Fourth Army had mounted an offensive in the Voibokalo direction and, on 9 December, Soviet forces liberated Tikhvin.

It then became possible to set in motion both the delivery of goods to Ladoga and the evacuation of people from Leningrad. It was still necessary to provide the ice road over the lake with reliable air cover, with anti-aircraft batteries, and with army detachments to cover it from the shore.

Still to come was the effective organization of the movement of vehicles and the smooth running of the operation: fuel and lubricating oil were in short supply and repair facilities were lacking. The road could not cope with the required volume of traffic and was failing to meet expectations. It was not until the latter part of December that it began to deliver some 700 to 800 tons of supplies to the city on a daily basis.

On 25 December Soviet troops gained possession of the Voibokalo sector, which allowed the work of restoring the railway to begin, which in turn enabled foodstuffs to be transported to Ladoga by rail and people to be evacuated by the same means.

A sense of the Leningraders' rapidly-dwindling reserves of strength spurred the men of the Fifty-Fourth Army on in their fight to recapture Tikhvin and inspired the lorry drivers and road maintenance crews alike to keep up a schedule of two or even three trips a day in their ramshackle thirty-hundredweight lorries, through the snowstorms and the snowdrifts.

16

The Final Pages

Yura's diary continues:

10 December 1941. The ten-day ration period is coming to an end. As for our evacuation, it is still an entirely open question. How agonizing this is! You are aware that, with every passing day, your strength is ebbing away, that day after day you are becoming more exhausted from malnutrition, and that the road that leads to death, death by starvation, is on a downward slope, so that the farther you go along it, the more accelerated this process of slow dying becomes. Yesterday, in the queue at the canteen, a woman was saying that five people in our building had already died of starvation... Meanwhile, planes are flying to Vologda! Each new arrival there is given a whole 800 grams of bread, and he can buy as much more as he wants for commercial prices. And butter too, and soup, and porridge, and a proper dinner. A dinner consisting not just of liquids, but containing solid ingredients, namely: porridge, bread, potatoes, vegetables... What a contrast with our Leningrad! If we could only wrench ourselves out of the monstrous embrace of this mortal hunger, if we could only break free from this constant fear for our lives, if we could start a new peaceful life in a small country village somewhere, forget the miseries that we have lived through... Ah well, there it is, my dream for today.

'What you want, you will surely get. What you seek, you will always find!' But when Lebedev-Kumach compiled the lyrics for this nice little song, he wasn't thinking straight. Popular wisdom gets it right: 'Man is tempered by adversity. It is only in adversity that a man's true character is fully revealed.' This applies to me too. Adversity hasn't tempered me, however, it has only weakened me, and this character of mine has proved to be egoistical. But I feel it is beyond my strength now to break the mould of my character. If I could just take the first step! Tomorrow, if everything goes the same way as it did this morning, I will have to fetch all the spice cakes home, but I'm sure I won't be able to resist eating at least a quarter of a spice cake. This is how my egoism reveals itself. However, I am going to try and bring them all home intact. All! All! All! All! All right, suppose I do slide down towards death by starvation, towards being bloated, waterlogged, I will at least have the satisfaction of knowing that I behaved honestly, that I have some willpower. Tomorrow I must demonstrate this willpower to myself, by not taking even a tiny piece from whatever I buy! Not a single little morsel! If the evacuation doesn't come off – though the hope of being evacuated is still alive in me – I will have to be capable of supporting Mother and Ira. There will be only one solution – to go and work as a hospital orderly. But I have already developed another plan. Mother will go to some newly-established hospital as a librarian, and I will be her assistant. Ira will stay with us.

This evening will bring me nothing but tears. I know it. Mother will come in hungry and cold. We are running out of firewood: we have almost none left. She will get nothing warm, nothing to eat either. She will be exhausted, overwrought. Smolny will either have given a negative response or the question will still be left open. She won't have managed to get any oilcake. This morning, before she went out, Ira had an attack of crying – a bad omen! Have I really begun to believe in omens? It seems that I have. What gloomy thoughts are creeping into my brain! Everything is bitter, every-thing is desolate, hunger and cold have taken over the world. All my thoughts are concentrated on just food and warmth. It is freezing hard outside – twenty to twenty-five degrees below zero. Although the stove has been alight, it is so cold in the room that my feet have frozen and there are shivers running up and down my spine. But just give me a loaf of bread to eat! I would revive, I would start to laugh, I would burst into song, I... but why go on?

The clock shows eleven in the morning. Ahead stretches the day, the evening, the night. And then... then comes a new day, a new ration of 125 grams of bread. A new ten-day ration period. Sweets... Life will fade away from me slowly, as slowly as the pages of this diary are being turned... But slowly and surely!

11 December 1941. I've been in such a foul mood both yesterday and today. Today I failed by a tiny margin to keep my word of honour – I took half a sweet from the ones I bought and I also took about forty grams of dried apricots from 200 grams. I hadn't actually given my word of honour about the dried apricots, but I had about the half a sweet. I ate it and I felt such a pang in my soul that I would have spat out the tiny piece I had eaten, but I couldn't make myself do it. And I also ate a tiny little piece of chocolate. Well, you can see what kind of a person I am! Yesterday one of Mother's legs swelled up badly. The question of the evacuation is still open: Mother hasn't been able to get herself included on any other evacuation list, so Smolny is our only hope. Smolny will bestow either life or death on the three of us, Mother, me and Ira. After today, we have only 200 to 300 grams of cereal left for the second ten-day period and 300 grams of meat. As for sweets, we have 650 grams in all, although it is true we should also get 200 grams of sugar on Ira's card. Mother's rations for the second ten-day period have already been half used up; in reserve there are only Ira's (150 grams) and mine (180 grams). And, to all outside appearances, we are preparing to be evacuated, getting our things together, getting ready to go...

I am no longer gladdened by the offensive that our troops have begun along the whole of the Front. Tikhvin has been recaptured, as has Yelets; in the Rostov direction the Germans are fleeing towards Mariupol and Taganrog; in the Moscow direction our troops are beginning to drive the Germans out of the areas that they had occupied. Due to a lack of de-icing fluid, hundreds of German aircraft are out of action, which is why the Germans are not bombing Leningrad these days; in Yugoslavia partisan warfare is being deployed on an increasingly broad scale; German forces are suffering heavy losses at the hands of the English in Libya; only Japan continues to defeat the USA, inflicting some extremely telling blows, but the same fate will be meted out to Japan as Germany will get from us. Oh, if only we could get permission to fly out! Only someone who has lived through great sorrow, great suffering, can appreciate to its full extent the kind of happiness that exists only here on earth. In two more ten-day periods it will be New Year. Who knows where we will be, what will have become of us? This New Year's Eve the traditional ornaments will lie forsaken inside the divan, there won't be any fir tree for them, nowhere for them to show off in all their glitter and finery. No one in Leningrad on that night will be in the mood for decorating a tree. If we are still alive, we will remember as though in a dream how New Year's Eve used to be in previous years: the fir tree with its candles aglow, the supper with its abundance of spicy things, tasty titbits and other kinds of sweetmeats, the sort you always have on hand for the New Year... We may do that, but anyway what's the good of trying to guess ahead, to guess what might happen to you? How will Tina spend that night? Where will her thoughts be at midnight precisely on 31 December 1941, when the final page of the calendar will be torn off and the new, clean, fresh calendar for 1942 opened up? Time is flying, flying...

At the moment Mother is out making enquiries about departures from Leningrad and seeing about the felt boots from her friend.

Anfissa Nikolaievna is pacing about angry and morose. It is easy to understand why. Her stocks of dried bread and cereal have come to an end, the day after tomorrow she will get her final allowance of milk from the tuberculosis clinic, and the question of evacuation still remains open for her as well. And so she is furious; she is afraid that she will go hungry. Well, one shouldn't laugh at the misfortunes of others. God grant that a time will come when all over the world there will be no one at all who knows what hunger is.

The pages in my diary are also coming to an end. It seems that

142

the diary itself is determining for me the length of time I will be keeping it.

12 December 1941. Mother has just left for the ration-card bureau. The whole of my future life hangs in the balance. If the story of the illegal ration card should surface, I might even do away with myself. It could certainly turn out that way. If that happened, for me, having grown up in an almost carefree, happy, and, as it seems to me now, an idyllic setting, to go on living then would mean constantly tormenting myself, until starvation or a German bullet put an end to my miserable existence. What would happen to Ira and to Mother then? Getting out of Leningrad, even flying out, if the answer from Smolny turned out to be positive, could only take place during the month of January. Whereas getting bloated and dying of water retention could happen within a week, and being dispatched into that other world by a stray splinter of shrapnel or some imminent chemical weapon could occur in a mere instant.

But I must not appear to be downhearted. Otherwise it would be the end. Not the end for me (for me the end will probably come in... well, I can't put an exact time on it, but at any moment), but the end for Mother and Ira. Tina will shed a tear in some faraway place, will remember all our past life, will feel some regret, then six months later she will be her old self again... Six months will pass, a year, the war will end, the former happy life of our city will return again. Our dead bodies will rot, our bones will crumble to dust, but Leningrad will stand on the banks of the Neva for all eternity, proud and invincible.

So many people are dying every day in Leningrad! So many deaths by starvation! It is only now that I can visualize for myself the reality of a city besieged by the enemy. Starvation brings death to every living being. Only those who have experienced famine for themselves can understand it. It is impossible for a person who has not had this experience to imagine it.

But why such sad thoughts, so much melancholy? Since we have been given life, this priceless gift of nature, why should we dwell on its bad aspects? Think only of the good things of life, take from it all the pleasures that it has to give. Why waste it?

All that is true, but there is some kind of hidden maggot gnawing secretly at my soul. Man is never entirely satisfied with the present alone. He also needs at least some prospect of improvement, no matter how meagre; something new for the future. It would be true to say that 'youth is nourished by hope', provided the saying were amended slightly to read: 'everyone is nourished by hope'.

Mother has not come home. In half an hour, or even a bit less, I will have to go to the company canteen. Incidentally, today is apparently the fourth anniversary of the elections to the Supreme Council of the USSR. Today I can state frankly that we wouldn't be able to hold out in Leningrad for more than a month. It's as plain as two plus two equals four. Just now there was a knock at the door. I ran to open it, my heart thumping with anxiety. I opened it... not Mother, but Anfissa Nikolaievna.

Five in the evening and no sign of Mother. This means something bad has happened. Either the business with the card has come to light and Mother has perhaps even been detained at the bureau, or else Mother has had a bad accident of some kind and is possibly already in a hospital by now or even a mortuary... Fate has no end of tricks to play!

And all this is because of that ration card. So why did Mother take the card? She took it because of me, because of my famished look. It was I who pushed her towards a criminal act, I who could well be to blame for Mother's death or at least for a miserable future life for Mother and Ira, for Tina's grief, to say nothing of the harm done to myself. I am to blame for all of it! If I hadn't sunk into melancholy, into depression, it would all have been different. It was under my influence that Mother turned to crime, I must take her punishment on myself. And if even that doesn't work, if I have ruined all our lives, then I will sacrifice my own life. I must and I can do it. I will volunteer for the People's Army, and at least do a good job at the Front, laying my life down for my country. To lay my life down, not omitting to pay my debt. 'As you make your bed, so you must lie on it.' 'As you sow, so shall you reap.'

144

If the story of the ration card has surfaced, I shall send an express telegram to Tina with the following message: 'Am dying. No help needed. Forget us. Yura.' Well, that's what I would have written if I were on my own. But there is Ira to think of. When all is said and done, wouldn't it be enough for me to have spoilt their whole lives? It is easy enough to die, but if I could set Ira on the right path! You write such things and it's all you can do not to weep! Yesterday Mother said: 'All my hope now is in God. Here I am, a Communist Party member, but I believe in God. Ira does too.' But God helps those who help themselves. And yet I feel that I may well be becoming religious too. I am looking at the icon and praying that God will avert this misfortune from us.

And Mother is still not here. By now it is well after five. She left early and she is not back yet. And there was definitely shelling somewhere today...

Tina, the only person who holds us dear, who would not forsake us in our hour of need, is far, far away, at Kansk in the Krasnoyarsky region, beyond the blockade, beyond the Front, beyond the Urals, beyond the Yenisey River, in the very depths of Siberia...

I will wait for another half an hour or an hour and then I will go and look for Mother. I must know where she is. And if I don't find her, tomorrow I will have to make enquiries at the hospitals, visit the mortuaries... What horrible things I am writing, I can't go on any more. My God! My God!

13 and 14 December 1941. I am writing for two days at once, which rarely happens to me nowadays. I spent half the day flat on my back in bed, then in the evening I went shopping and bought six slabs of cocoa with sugar made from soya at thirty roubles apiece (each slab weighing 100 grams) and also 300 grams of cheese at nineteen roubles a kilo. On my way home there was an unfortunate occurrence, with the result that I arrived home with only 350 grams of the cocoa, plus the cheese. There was a scene with Mother and Ira. Mother, having got back from the District Party Committee, informed us that we had been put on the list of those to be evacuated by lorry in the Ministry of Construction convoy which, according to the assurances of both the District Party Committee and the District Council, is due to leave between 15 and 20 December. It seems that the question of flying out will also be settled tomorrow. There is no food in the house at all, except for 100 grams of bread, which Mother got in exchange for a packet of tobacco. I have toothache, I feel generally unwell, somehow I don't believe in this departure from Leningrad, I can think of nothing but food, I can barely stay on my feet, so that, in spite of the news about being evacuated and the good news from the Front (the rout of the German armies near Moscow, Rostov and Tikhvin), I am in a depressed frame of mind. If I could only fortify myself with something, eat something! I'm sure I would revive...

15 December 1941. Each day that I live through here is a day that brings me closer to suicide. There is really no way out. It's a dead end, I can't go on living like this any longer. Hunger. Dreadful hunger. Everything about the evacuation has gone silent again. It is becoming hard to go on living. To go on living, not knowing what for, to go on living, dragging out your existence in hunger and cold. With temperatures of twenty-five to thirty degrees below zero, the cold penetrates even felt boots within ten minutes. I can't... Mother and Ira are here beside me. I can't take their piece of bread away from them. I can't do it, because I know what even a crumb of bread means nowadays. But I can see how they share theirs with me, while I, miserable swine that I am, sneak their last scraps on the sly. And what have they been reduced to, if yesterday Mother could say to me with tears in her eyes that she sincerely wished I had choked on the little makeweight of bread (about ten to fifteen grams) that I had pinched from her and Ira. What a terrible thing this hunger is! I feel, I know, that if someone offered me some deadly poison, which would bring me a death without suffering, in my sleep, I would take it and be thankful. I want to live, but I can't live like this! But I do want to live! What am I to do?

Where is Mother? Where is she?

Well, this is really it... I have lost my integrity, lost my belief in it. I have reached the end of the road. Two days ago I was sent to get our sweets. It was bad enough that instead of sweets I bought sweetened cocoa (counting on Ira not wanting to eat it and so increasing my share), but as well as that I helped myself to half of the total amount – a miserable 600 grams supposed to last us for the whole of the ten-day period – and invented a story about how three packets of cocoa had been snatched from my hands. I acted out the comedy at home with tears in my eyes and I gave Mother my word of honour as a Pioneer that I had not taken a single packet of cocoa for myself... And later on, watching with a hardened heart Mother's tears and distress at being deprived of something sweet, I ate the cocoa surreptitiously. Today, on my way back from the bread shop, I took a little extra piece of bread weighing about twenty-five grams from Mother and Ira's rations and ate that on the sly too. Just now, in the canteen, I ate a bowl of crab soup, a main rissole dish, and one and a half helpings of fruit soup. I took home to Mother and Ira just one and a half helpings of fruit soup and at home I again took a part of their share for myself.

I have slid down into that abyss called depravity, where the voice of conscience is totally silent, where there is dishonesty and disgrace. I am an unworthy son to my mother and an unworthy brother to my sister. I am an egoist, a person who, in a moment of adversity, forgets all about his nearest and dearest. And, while I am behaving like this, Mother is straining herself to breaking point. With swollen legs, with heart trouble, wearing summer shoes in the freezing weather, without so much as a crust of bread during the day, she is running around the various organizations, making the most pathetic attempts, trying to wrench us out of here. I have lost my belief in the evacuation. It has ceased to exist for me. As far as I am concerned, the entire world has turned into food. Everything that is left has food as its purpose, getting it, receiving it...

I am a ruined person. Life is over for me. The prospect that lies ahead of me is not life. I would like two things to happen immediately: for myself to die, here and now, and for Mother to read through this diary. May she curse me as a filthy, unfeeling and hypocritical creature, let her renounce me… I have sunk too low, too low…

What will happen next? Could it be that death won't take me? I would welcome a quick death, not an agonizing one, not the death by starvation that has been standing like a bloody spectre so close ahead.

It is so sad, so shameful, so pitiful to look at Ira…

Will I really commit suicide? Will I really do it?

Something to eat! Food!

24 December 1941. For a whole eight days I have not picked up my pen.

There have been some changes in me. It seems to me that something good has made an appearance in my character. The stimulus for this was provided by my losing Ira's ration card for sugar. Oh, how despicably I behaved towards Mother and Ira on that occasion! My attention wandered for a moment in the shop and I lost 200 grams of sugar, 100 grams of chocolate for Ira and Mother and 150 grams of sweets. I want to change, I want to forge a new character for myself, but I feel that, without support from Mother and Ira, I wouldn't last long in my honest new life. Let them be there to soften things somehow – well, I don't know how to express it more clearly. Today, for the first time in many days now, I brought home all the sweets I had bought on ration in the canteen and I am sharing the bread equally with Ira and Mother, although I do sometimes still steal a crumb on the sly. But today I felt such a warm attitude towards me on Mother and Ira's part when they separated a bit out for me from their own share of sweets – a quarter of a sweet from Mother (although she took it back again later) and half a sweet from Ira, to thank me for making the trip to the canteen for spice cakes, sweets and oilcake flatbread – that I almost burst into tears. And these are the very people I was deceiving so badly earlier, and who now know about my deceitful behaviour! It all goes to show what can be done with a better attitude! But, on the other hand, that same Mother took a spice cake from me, promising an extra sweet in return (having had an extra sweet herself), and that same Ira cried because Mother had given us both a sweet each, and then I gave Ira some of my own sweet, so that in the end Ira ate more sweets than I did. To tell the truth, I sinned today too: I hid one of the spice cakes from Mother and Ira... Well, that's how bad it is...

Mother has been given some sort of a promise by the District Party Committee that she will be evacuated on 28 December. Mother has now gone to the Committee to discuss the matter. If the evacuation happened to be postponed until 1 January, we are doomed, because we only have coupons left for two days, just possibly for three. Not more.

Mother's health is going from bad to worse. The swelling has now extended to her thighs. I am completely infested with lice. Ira and I are slightly bloated in the face. Today we finished off the sweets. Tomorrow it will be the cereal. The day after tomorrow, the meat and butter. And after that, after that...

A silent, oppressive sadness. Heavy and painful. Grief and a weighty, mournful sorrow. Perhaps even more than that. I only recall the days, the evenings spent here when I emerge from the kitchen into our apartment. In the kitchen there is still a sort of mirage of our old pre-war life. A political map of Europe on the wall, kitchen utensils, sometimes an open book on the table waiting to be read, a pendulum clock on the wall, warmth from the stove, when it is alight. But I want to go round the whole apartment again. I put on a padded jacket, a hat, fasten my belt, pull mittens over my hands, and I open the door leading into the corridor. It is freezing cold out there. Dense clouds of vapour stream from my mouth, the cold penetrates even beneath my collar, I shiver involuntarily. The corridor is empty. There are four of her chairs piled on top of one another, left there by Anfissa Nikolaievna, and shelves from the wardrobe, split into firewood, lean against the wall. Three rooms used to be ours. Now we are allowed to occupy only two of them. The one nearest to the kitchen is occupied by Anfissa's family. There is no point in discussing them. In their room there is a little metal stove burning merrily away, the smell of something appetizing is wafting out from under their door, the faces of the occupants of this room are lit with happiness, with a sense of repletion. And next to it... an empty room, papered in brown; the window has been broken, a cold wind from the street is circulating round the room; there is a bare oak table against the wall and an empty *étagère* in the corner. Dust and cobwebs all over the walls... What is it? It is what used to be our dining room, a joyful place, somewhere to study, somewhere for us to relax. Once upon a time (it seems long, long ago) there used to be a sofa standing there, a dresser, chairs, an unfinished meal on the table, books on the *étagère*, and I would be stretched out on the sofa reading *Les Trois Mousquetaires*, while enjoying a snack of white bread, butter and cheese or else munching chocolate. It used to be warm in the room and, to quote Pushkin, I was 'always satisfied with myself, my dinner and my wife' – well, I didn't have that last commodity but, to make up for it, there were games, books, magazines, chess, the cinema... and I would fret if I hadn't managed to get to the theatre or some such thing, and I often went without dinner until the evening, preferring to play volleyball with my comrades. And, finally, how well I remember the Leningrad Pioneer Palace, the evenings spent there, the reading room, the games, the history club, the chess club, the puddings they used to serve in the canteen, the concerts, the dances... This was happiness, and I didn't even realize it at the time – the happiness of living in the USSR in a time of peace, the happiness of having a mother and an aunt taking care of me, of knowing that no one would snatch my future away from me. This was true happiness. And the room next door – it is a gloomy, cheerless storeroom in semi-darkness, crammed with the various belongings remaining to us. A chest of drawers, dismantled bedsteads, two desks, one on top of the other, a divan – all covered in dust, all shut up, packed away, ready to lie there for thousands of years if need be...

The cold, the bitter cold, drove us out of this room as well. But once there was an electric hotplate there, with an omelette cooking on it or sausages, soup being heated. Mother used to sit at the table and work long into the night by the light of a table lamp.

150

There used to be a gramophone playing there, the sound of joyful laughter, a huge fir tree reaching right to the ceiling would be put up, ablaze with candles. Tina would come to visit us, my friend Mishka would come; on the table there would be piles of sandwiches (which had just about everything in them!), on the tree there would be dozens of sweets hanging, and spice cakes (which nobody ever ate), there was just about everything you could think of! But now it is a desolate place, or so it seems, cold and dark, and there is no reason for me to be looking into this room.

The kitchen, the kitchen alone, is the place where our domestic life is led. It is there that we eat (provided we have something to put in our mouths), there that we warm ourselves (provided we have something to put in the stove), there that we sleep (when the lice let up a little on their biting), there that we have established our little nook.

The apartment has become an empty shell. All the life in it has faded away. It is as if it had frozen, turned into an icicle, and it will not thaw until the spring.

3 January 1942. This is almost the last entry in the diary. I am afraid that even this one... I don't think that it will fall to me to finish off this diary of mine, to write the words 'The End' on the last page. It will be someone else who will note the word 'Dead' on it. But I so passionately want to live, to believe, to feel! However, the evacuation is not due to take place until the spring, when trains will begin to move along the Northern railway, and I won't last until the spring. I have become waterlogged, each cell of my tissues contains more water than it should. Consequently, all my internal organs must be bloated. I am reluctant to move from one place to another, reluctant to get up from my chair, to go anywhere. But all this comes from an excess of water and a lack of food. It is all liquid, liquid, liquid! I am so swollen.

Mother and Ira have broken off with me. They will leave me behind. Mother's nervous system is in such a state by now that she is ready to lose control, and then... As has already happened, as she tells me every day, she and Ira will get out of here somehow, but

151

I won't. Am I some kind of a worker? Am I some kind of a student? Well, I would work, I would study for a week, and then I would kick the bucket. Is that the way it will be? Death, death is staring me right in the face. And there is nowhere to hide from it. Perhaps I could go to a hospital – but I am covered in lice. Lord, what should I do? I will die, I will die for sure, but I so much want to live, to get away, to live, to live! But perhaps Ira at least will stay alive. Oh, how heavy my heart is… Mother is so rude to me nowadays, sometimes she hits me, and I get cursing from her at every turn. But I am not angry with her for that. I can see that I am a parasite, hanging round her and Ira's necks. Yes, death, death is up ahead. And there is no hope at all, only the fear that I will force my own mother and sister to perish with me.

4 January 1942. And still a whole month lies ahead before the food situation will improve and before the day of departure. What will have become of us by the end of this month, what kind of paupers will we have turned into, unless some outstanding gift of fortune tears us away from here, unless the mercy of God or divine salvation gets us evacuated tomorrow or the day after, before the middle of the second ten-day period? Only God, if such exists, can give us deliverance. Let Him save us now, then never, ever will I have to lie to my mother again, never will I have to soil my honest name, it will become sacred to me again. Oh, if only we could be evacuated, right now! And I vow with my whole life that I will put an end to my disgraceful, cheating life for ever, I will begin an honest and hard-working life in some village, I will give Mother the gift of a happy and golden old age. Only a belief in God, only a belief that luck won't forsake me or the three of us tomorrow, a belief in a reply from the District Party Committee, saying: 'You may go!' – only this would get me on my feet. Otherwise I am done for. But I want to survive or, rather, I would like to, but I can't – I just need to leave tomorrow. I will be capable of repaying Mother and Ira with good in my behaviour towards them. Lord, just save me, get me evacuated, save all three of us, Mother and Ira and me!

6 January 1942. I am almost completely unable either to walk or to work. An almost complete lack of strength. Mother can hardly walk either – I can't even imagine how she is managing to get about. Nowadays she often hits me, swears at me, shouts at me. She gets wild nervous attacks, she can't bear my worthless appearance – the appearance of a person frail from lack of strength, starving, exhausted, who can barely move from one place to another, who gets in the way and 'pretends' to be ill and feeble. But I truly am not faking my weakness. No! It is no pretence. My strength is leaving me, leaving, ebbing away... And time drags by, drags by, so long-drawn-out, so very long! Oh, Lord, what is happening to me?

And now I, I, I...

And so the moment came – the day of the evacuation. The few things that were needed for the journey and the belongings that could be carried had been placed on a little sled. Yura got up from his bed, looked for his stick, tried to stand, but couldn't. He was unable to and fell back onto his bed.

17

Remaining Human

Even during the most intense privations, a small act of human kindness could brighten another person's life – sometimes even save it. As Ludmila Nikolaievna Bokshitskaya recalls:

I survived the siege in the most severe manner: without reserves, without help, but in the belief that it would come to an end before long. But the moment came – it was in December 1941 – when we simply lost interest: we were unable to make ourselves go to collect our bread ration, we didn't get out of our beds. Three people just lying there: my mother, my sister and myself. We didn't react to the air-raid warnings, we didn't hear the bombers flying overhead. But, as they say, 'Everyone had his own personal saviour'.

Our neighbour, Nadezhda Sergeievna Kuprianova, entered our room. She had convinced herself that we must already be dead, because there was no longer anyone else left alive in the apartment, where once there had been a number of residents. Seeing that we had 'turned our faces to the wall', that we had already become indifferent to our own situation, Nadezhda Sergeievna declared that she was not going to allow the family of such a wonderful woman to perish, and left the room. Soon she returned with some firewood. She lit the stove, brought some water. Saying that she had been given a rabbit at the hospital, she put a pan with the rabbit in it on the stove. While the soup was cooking, she washed us, having hung a blanket to shield us from the worst of the cold. In those days our corner room on the first floor had frozen through to such

154

an extent that it was warm only by the stove, within a one-metre radius. It was only after the meal that we found out that it had been a cat, probably the very last one, not a rabbit. This meal and this neighbourly concern allowed us to keep our heads above water until 10 January 1942.

On 8 and 9 January, again without any feeling for what was going on around us, we two daughters had been lying down with our mother, fully dressed, not having gone to claim our bread ration, but this time we weren't talking about it as we had done before. Mother began to stir, to ask something quietly in her sleep, or so it seemed to me. And then Mother, as though jerked awake, asked the question: 'What day is it today?' And, based on the fact that we had not gone for bread for two days, we concluded that it was 10 January 1942. And suddenly Mother said that we could not allow ourselves to die on a day which had such happy associations for her, it being Ludmila's birthday, that is to say, mine. We must get ourselves up that day and find work clearing away snow. She had evidently heard on the radio that workers were needed.

And nowadays I count that date, not just as a new birthday for me, but also as a joint birthday shared with my mother and my sister. We set off for Skorokhodov Street, where the centre for work placement was. At first we would take three steps and then stop, but not for long, then ten steps... I remember how we kept count, so as not to exceed the number, afraid that we would not be able to manage; how, when we stopped, we were very watchful to avoid getting frost-bitten...

People did their utmost, even during the darkest days of the siege, to continue marking in some way important family occasions such as birthdays. Given their extremely limited resources, this could require some ingenuity, as Svetlana Alexandrovna Tikhomirova recounts:

I was wanting to give my mother a gift of some kind for her birthday on 25 March 1942, to buy her something, me being fourteen years old at the time. There was no loaf or lump sugar to be had, but there was granulated sugar. I don't remember what the

155

ration was. In the mornings, when we drank our tea, Mother would tip some granulated sugar into saucers, for my father, for me, and for herself. And I had to separate out a part of my share in some inconspicuous way, sometimes pouring it into my fist, sometimes leaving it on the saucer, sometimes putting it in my pocket and then tipping it out somewhere. I had this little antique bowl. I collected the granulated sugar in it. It probably took about two months to do it – it didn't always work. My father pretended not to notice, and when Mother went over to the stove to pour the tea – that's when I would tip the sugar in. In those days we always had some glue soaking in soup bowls on the windowsill – it was the kind shaped like a bar of chocolate, it took several days for it to soak. And we had this glue for breakfast, for dinner. I kept the granulated sugar hidden. Whenever my gaze chanced on it, I always had the urge to stick my finger in it and taste it. There was one occasion when I felt like getting up at night and going over to the bowl in my bare feet.

When the big day came, I remember being highly excited – my palms were actually damp with sweat. I needed to get up earlier than Mother. I put the bowl full of granulated sugar on the table: probably 300 grams had accumulated! Well, needless to say, there were tears. The sugar was immediately shared out again. And that's how the birthday was celebrated...

That saddest of family occasions, the burial of a loved one, became increasingly difficult to arrange as public services ceased to function, the ground froze hard, and there were few people left with the strength to dig a grave. Yevdokiya Nikolaievna Filonova, the sister of the gifted Soviet painter Pavel Nikolaievich Filonov, describes her brother's death and burial:

In the autumn of 1941, towards the end of October, my brother paid us an unexpected visit. He arrived bringing four tiny potatoes. He was bringing them at a time when they were literally worth their weight in gold. He was depriving his wife, Yekaterina Alexandrovna, and himself at a time when everyone was starving. They had no reserves of food at all.

156

When Molotov made his speech about the outbreak of war over the radio on 22 June 1941, I called my brother and asked him to get in a stock of food. He said irritatedly: 'If people like you and me start building up reserves, it would be criminal.' But, perhaps, if he had thought otherwise, he might not have died so soon, just six months after the declaration of war.

It was extremely cold. He was wearing his jacket, a warm hat and a pair of his son's ski-ing trousers (no doubt Yekaterina Alexandrovna had insisted on him putting these trousers on over his own cotton ones, which he wore summer and winter alike).

No matter how adamantly we refused the tiny potatoes, however insistently we asked him to take them back, he wouldn't even hear of it, he remained determined that we should accept them. Unfortunately, I no longer remember now what we talked about then. It was very cold indeed in our house. He didn't take off his outdoor things, he didn't stay with us long. It's possible that he was thinking that this might be his last visit to us, but it never occurred to us that we might be seeing him for the last time. And now I can't take it in, I can't forgive myself for not taking those potatoes back to them, for keeping them ourselves. Having closed the door behind him, we went over to the window, expecting that, as he always used to, he would stop, wave his hand to us in farewell, and smile – but that time it didn't happen. He walked across the courtyard with his usual big strides, but slowly, with his head bent low. When he had disappeared under the archway, we just stayed by the window, looking at one another in dismay.

What was he thinking about then? What was he feeling?

That was his last visit to us.

My brother had volunteered to help protect the apartment building in which he lived from incendiary bombs for the duration of the war. Starving hungry, how cold he must have been in his jacket which, because of the cold, could never be removed, not even indoors. Once he fell down the stairs in the dark. He wouldn't send for a doctor, relying, as usual, on his own resources. But he ran out of resources... I don't know how it was on that occasion, but, normally, if he fell ill (and he very rarely fell ill), he would sit in an armchair and doze, but he wouldn't take to his bed. To tell the truth, it would have been a hard bed for even a healthy person to lie on, let alone an invalid (he slept with no mattress on his bed). He had no faith in either doctors or medicines.

On the morning of 3 December 1941 we received word that my brother had been taken gravely ill. We rushed to him immediately. The trams were still running. When we entered the room, we saw my brother lying on the bed, which was not in its usual place. He was lying in his jacket, wearing a warm hat. On his left hand there was a white woollen mitten, on his right hand there was none – he was clutching it in his fist. His breathing was inaudible. In profound silence, not talking at all, we waited for the doctor to come, to give some kind of injections. But, even before his arrival, we realized that it was all over. He had been breathing so quietly and so slowly that we had failed to notice his dying breath. He had left us so quietly…

On the day of the burial, we – my sister and I – obtained two sledges and brought them along: a big one and a child's one, the latter for Yekaterina Alexandrovna, because she was unable to walk behind the coffin. They were to accompany my brother's body to the cemetery without me, because my job was to arrange for the place where his body was to be brought a few hours later. Having arrived at the Serafimovskoye Cemetery, I found the man who, for some bread and a given sum of money, had agreed to get the place ready. What inhuman labour it was! It remained bitterly cold, the earth hard as stone. But, even more than by the frost, the work was hindered by the roots of an acacia, near where he had to dig the earth. And, as I remember it – and it is impossible to forget – he spent more time hacking at the roots with an axe than working with the spade. Eventually I couldn't stand it any longer and I told him that I was going to help him, but about five minutes later he took the spade from me and said: 'It is beyond your strength.' How afraid I was that he would abandon the job or that, even though going on with the work, he would start cursing and swearing! But all he said was: 'Normally I would have dug three graves in this time.' I could not add anything to the amount we had agreed on –

I had with me only just enough to pay him for his work – but I said to him: 'If only you knew what kind of a man you are toiling for!' And in answer to his question: 'Who is he?' I told him about my brother's life, how he had worked for the benefit of others, taught people, receiving nothing in return for his enormous efforts. While continuing with his work, he listened to me very attentively. I can still see that man extremely clearly even now, and it seems to me that I would recognize him if I met him. He was not a cemetery worker, but had been reduced to this hard labour in order to feed his family. And how grateful I am to him for his hard work, for doing that awful job patiently and, above all, without cursing and swearing.

When they brought in my brother's body, everything was ready...

One of the authors of this book, Daniil Granin, was fighting on the Leningrad Front during the winter months of 1941-1942 and remembers the boost to morale given by an unexpected visit from a group of Leningrad women factory workers bringing gifts for the troops:

We were stationed near Pushkin. Our detached artillery and machine-gun battalion was occupying a sector beyond the railway line, a bare, snow covered, low-lying area. The sector was much too big for a single battalion. There were almost no reinforcements arriving. Sometimes there were no more than five or seven men left in a platoon. There were not enough personnel to mount a full guard and we could not relieve those manning the outposts. And every day we had to clear the communication passages of snow. And the trenches. And clear the field of fire. We had to find wood from somewhere, to haul it to the dugouts, to stoke the stoves, to clean our weapons. Given that, on top of everything else, we were also busy shooting, standing guard, dragging the wounded to the other side of the railway embankment... And besides all that, we used to crawl into no man's land at break of day to retrieve cabbages from beneath the snow, because we were starving hungry. Someone was sent off to hospital every day, either with frostbite or with oedema.

159

Nowadays it is no longer possible to understand how we were able to hold the line of defence, go out on reconnaissance, and even try to win back high ground. Basically, we lived in a very restricted space – the platoon command dugout, the forward outpost, to the left a broken-down, burnt-out thirty-hundredweight lorry, covered in snow, which had ended up in the middle of a field, nobody knew how; to the right in the distance were the Pulkovo Heights and, nearer to us, nothing but bushes. As for what lay ahead, directly in front of us was Pushkin railway station and, through binoculars, Catherine's Palace could be seen. And that was our whole landscape, our front line, our field of battle. We knew little about what was happening in neighbouring sectors. But the Germans, on the other hand, were stationed right beside us, so we had ample opportunity to study them, get to know them and see them; in places our trenches were so close to theirs that we could hear what they were saying to one another, the clinking of their thermos flasks. When one of our snipers managed to shoot a Jerry, we could hear them yelling and cursing.

Ahead of us were the Germans, behind us Leningrad was in sight. In the clear air the silhouette of the city stood out distinctly, with all its spires, domes and chimneys, as though it had been etched by an old master craftsman on the rim of the earth, between the white fields and the blue sky. At night the crimson reflections of fires ate away at the city. By day shells flew over our heads with a soft swishing sound. The sky was empty, but we could hear their invisible flight and then, after a delay, the dull thud of their explosions would reach our ears. The Germans shelled the city according to a regular schedule, and their bombers flew over the city on a regular schedule too. Their return flight path was above our heads. At one time, out of impotent fury, we would fire our rifles at them, we would fire armour-piercing bullets, we would fire the anti-tank guns, in the hope of hitting some unprotected, vulnerable spot. That was a long time back. Later on we got wiser, and we were also saving our cartridges for more serious business. We simply kept track of how the anti-aircraft batteries would begin to fire above the city and how the bombing was going. Black columns of smoke would slowly rise, distorting the city's clear-cut profile. We tried to make out which area of the city was under bombardment.

We were unable to do anything about it. The only thing we could do was not to look back at Leningrad. And we were not eager to go into the city. In any case, they didn't let us go there very often. I myself went there only once during that winter, for instance, and that was enough for me. But all the same we were constantly aware of the presence of the city behind our backs, felt its ragged, barely audible breathing. There was nothing like it on any other front line.

From the day we heard about the crushing defeat of the Germans outside Moscow, everything changed for us. The fighting was still going badly for us there on the Leningrad Front, our December-January offensive failed, we had little to show for all our efforts, we were not yet capable of launching effective offensive attacks. But, in spite of all that, we somehow became utterly convinced that the Germans would not take Leningrad. Not because they lacked the resources to do so, but because we would not allow them to. This extraordinary conviction, apparently without any solid foundation, gripped us in those December days, the very days of our weakness, starvation and lack of manpower. It was possibly linked in some way to the fact that a delegation of Leningrad women factory workers came to visit our front-line detachment in the latter part of December, to present us with some gifts. Perhaps the authorities had decided that our fighting spirit would be of support to the Leningraders, or perhaps those in command intended the visit to inspire us – I don't know which. The delegation reached our company in the form of three women. All three of them were bundled up in headscarves and mufflers, belted, buckled and laced up. In the dugout, once they had finally freed themselves of their outer clothing, they were transformed into thin young women – you might almost say bony ones, judging from their jutting collar bones and cheek bones. The dugout was warmly heated, we entered and received from their hands gifts of socks, tobacco pouches and mittens. Their dresses hung loosely from their bony little shoulders – they were much too big for them – but they each seemed sweet to us. They had arrived at our place in the evening, when it was dark outside. An hour later a sergeant brought in our porridge. The pot of porridge with salt meat and a lump of sugar – that was our dinner, our supper too, and those who could, kept back a bit for their breakfast. We also had bread and dried bread. That evening we shared our porridge with our guests, meaning that we gave it all to them in fact, so that each of them received almost two helpings. Then Volodya played his guitar for them. They told us about how they sewed underwear in a factory and then they fell asleep. Actually, they had begun to doze off immediately after they had eaten. They were tired from the journey, but mostly they were drowsy from the effects of the food and the warmth. They slept on our trestle beds. People came from neighbouring platoons to look into our dugout – to see for themselves. It seemed that it had been years since we had seen women in dresses. But what women these were! Skinny, exhausted, neglected looking. Crowding in the entrance to the dugout, the soldiers looked at the sleeping women with a feeling in which there was no trace of anything masculine, there was only compassion. But, on the other hand, this was probably the very essence of true masculinity. Those three women personified Leningrad for us...

We woke them up before morning came, so that they could get away while it was still dark. They would have liked to sleep longer, and assured us that they had not slept so soundly in recent months as they had with us on the front line.

The lieutenant and I accompanied them to the checkpoint. We took our bearings as we walked from the crimson-gold glow of the fires. A solitary searchlight was probing low down in the sky. The lieutenant invited them to the skating rink in the Central Park of Culture and Leisure next winter. 'You will recognize me by your nice little mittens,' he joked. I laughed with them and suddenly I understood: it was not going to work for the Germans, they would never enter the city. All that mattered now was how soon we would be able to throw them out.

18

I Am in a Frantic Hurry to Live!

Kniazev's diary continues:

3 January 1942. The 196th day of the war. I slowly climb the stairs. My heart is thumping. I allow up to ten seconds for each stair. Here at last is our front door on the third floor landing. I ring as arranged: three short, sharp rings. With an anxious heart I strain to hear my wife's footsteps. She is at home and expecting me. My heroic woman! She is uncomplainingly and stoically enduring each and every tribulation, hunger being the first and foremost. How thin she has become! As if she were not a woman of fifty-one, but a frail, slender young girl. I kiss her, I share her feelings, my dear, close wife and companion. She has lost none of her femininity, nor her exceptional feminine neatness. Her dark eyes are shining in her emaciated face. And I look at her with more emotion than a love-struck young man gazing at his beloved. What a heroine she has proved herself to be! I have known her as wife and friend for twenty-four and a half years, but I never suspected that she had within her such a reserve of spiritual energy and the willpower to overcome all obstacles. She has lost neither her goodwill towards other people, nor her cheerful, sunny disposition, nor her smile, nor the serene, inner depth of her captivating dark eyes. A marvellous Russian woman or, to be more precise, a woman who is Russian by her culture but who, by her birth, her nature, her integrity, her exceptional truthfulness and her honesty is a Zyrian: her mother and father were both Zyrians. This remarkable people, under pressure from more warlike, brutal and coarse nations, was pushed out into the taiga and the tundra, nearly to the very shores of the boundless, icy sea. When I was still a little boy, I read in a geography textbook: 'Zyrians are notable for their characteristic integrity.' This has turned out to be true. My dear, honest, pure wife and friend! How happy I am that we are together and at home!

In the hallway, where we have taken to living, the little lamp is twinkling. The stove is alight. We are starting our dinner: a bowlful of water with some kind of cereal in it and some pellets of black flour mixed with husks. Two or three scraps of dried bread, each weighing some ten or fifteen grams, looking when bought like lumps of putty. And nothing else for today. My wife's dream is that, in my capacity as Director of the Archives of the USSR Academy of Sciences and Vice Chairman of the Committee for the History of the Academy of Sciences, I will eventually obtain a top category ration card – a worker's one, that is – which we have petitioned for, and which would put me on a par at least with Urmancheieva, our cleaner lady and boiler-room attendant.

We don't dwell particularly on food problems; my wife and I are discussing the fact that Shakhmatova and her son Aliyosha have become utterly weak and are near to death; that, in a courtyard near the Archives, some unfortunate soul who had died of dystrophy had lain by the window all night long and had already had the boots stolen from his feet; that several items of food that we were due on our rations in December we never succeeded in finding for sale anywhere. My wife is taking comfort from the thought that they are at last going to open up a food distribution point at the Academy itself. But, in spite of all her efforts, she can no longer go on eating the pellets of black flour mixed with husks that they distributed in December instead of cereal. And I am struggling to finish mine, mostly so as not to upset her... And so our meal comes to an end.

5 January 1942. The 198th day of the war. Shakhmatova and her sixteen year old son Aliyosha have died from exhaustion and the ordeals they have undergone. The boy, Academician Shakhmatov's grandson, was a great enthusiast for the study of astronomy and was exceptionally gifted in that area. He would undoubtedly have distinguished himself in his beloved field of study in future years and would most likely have become an outstanding scientist and possibly even an academician. This news has been a terrible blow for both me and all our colleagues.

6 January 1942. The 199th day of the war. I presented my paper 'The history of the chairmanship of the Academy of Sciences during the whole period of its existence (1725-1941)' to a scientific meeting of the Committee for the History of the Academy of Sciences.

It could well be that this was my final scientific presentation.

13 and 14 January 1942. The 206th and 207th days of the war. Yesterday and today they have been broadcasting over the radio a speech by Popkov: 'All the worst is behind us. Ahead of us lies the liberation of Leningrad and the deliverance of the Leningraders from death by starvation.' Or so the content of the speech is being transmitted from mouth to mouth. I didn't hear it myself: our radio is not working.

People are living on their last hopes. We will probably pull through January, they are saying, but, unless there is some improvement, we won't survive February. Those who weaken just go on dying.

18 January 1942. The 211th day of the war. Since people are collapsing all around me, I too have begun to put my affairs and my papers in order, just in case. Today I finished the systematization of all my materials, on paper to begin with; I will arrange all my files within this framework.

19 January 1942. The 212th day of the war. In the Leningrad sector of the Institute of History, research fellows are dying one after the other. Lavrov, a fellow-student of mine at university, has died. Like me, he worked for the Central Archives, then he moved over to work at the Academy of Sciences. For some time he has been in charge of the History Archives at the Leningrad Institute of History. He was an exceptionally modest man, but somehow badly adapted to life. He crossed the dreadful line at the beginning of January. Having grown weak, he lay helplessly moribund, until his life was finally cut short.

Yesterday my wife confessed to me that she had grown weary. She has indeed got very thin, and these last few days she has grown pale as well. It is only her eyes, dark as ever, that glow with a shining light.

How much of our strength have we lost, what border have we reached? Where is the line – that dreadful line – which, once crossed, a person can never step back over? Taking our normal state as being 100 per cent, we decided that the dreadful line should be drawn at 50 per cent of our life force, and my wife defines her position at between 40 and 50 per cent, which is close to the dreadful line.

21 and 22 January 1942. The 214th and 215th days of the war. For the second day running I haven't been to work because of the intense cold; my wheelchair isn't working, the axle grease freezes. My wife is unable to accompany me there and back; her strength is noticeably weakening and it is only her spirit that is robust.

Can it be that we won't last until the spring? Far too many people are dying around us, and it is not happening elsewhere, but close to us, in our home, at work. Each of us can hear the swish of the scythe. I am reluctant to raise my eyes to the ceiling: there is a hook there, such a sturdy one, which caught my eye when I first entered the room some twelve years ago. The dreadful thought flashed through my mind then: will it ever be put to use? If anything should happen to my wife, it might well be put to use.

But who knows how fate will turn out? No one knows what will happen, not just tomorrow, but today, this very moment.

While I was arranging my papers, my various unpublished, completed and hardly-started works, I lovingly opened some of my favourite books and read from them.

31 January 1942. The 224th day of the war. The last day of a hard month. I keep alive because I have thoughts, plans. It is impossible to read in this semi-darkness, so I am mentally reviewing my course on the history of culture. If I survive the war, I will definitely announce this course of lectures at the University. Like those who always put a brave face on things, so I too, when in the presence of other people, try to stay smiling, to utter only optimistic words, to raise people's spirits. It is not for nothing that Academician Alexeievich has called me a 'great optimist'. It is only here, in these pages, that I allow myself free rein. I am completely myself here.

I met Svikul, whose fifteen year old son Vova, an unassuming lad, has just died. Inconsolable grief, despair – these words are pathetically inadequate compared with what her eyes, her sunken cheeks and trembling chin express. I embraced her, held her close – it was all I could do.

3 February 1942. The 227th day of the war. My wife returned empty handed from the food distribution centre. They are not giving out anything at all today.

Let's get away from our nightmarish present and explore some byway. Yesterday evening I put in some good work studying the past history of Asia Minor and the Hittite culture, alternating this occupation with work on my history of the Academy of Sciences. Let's get away again today.

Just a few more words for the future reader of these lines. Even within my own small world, certain personalities exist. In my neighbours' kitchen, where all of them are living now, there sits a 'defence lady', meaning the wife of an engineer engaged in the defence industry. She is in a position to acquire things in exchange for bread, cereal, butter and pork skin. She confines herself to the choicest items: underwear, shoes, table-linen, towels and, in exchange for such things, she gives, for instance, one kilo of bread for a large, well-kept carpet; a handful of millet and a few pieces of sugar for a lamp; 500 grams of rice for a pair of shoes... Our starving neighbours have only this resource to keep them going. As for the lady, she is not feeling the pinch... Which goes to show that, amongst those of us who are starving in Leningrad, there are some well-fed people too!

And here is a fragment of our everyday life for you. At the Archives today there were only two people present for duty, representing the day shift (as I have already mentioned, we had to cancel night duty because of the physical debility of the staff and the lack of heating fuel). A.I. Andreyev, a doctor of history, and Faina Urmancheieva, the boiler-room attendant and cleaner at the Archives – the wife of the boiler man who was called up for the army – were sitting near the stove in Room 12. Andreyev was reading Bauer's doctoral dissertation in preparation for its public defence. Faina was feeding the stove and getting bored. Andreyev tried to make her laugh about something and then went on with his reading. Faina, the mother of three children, is a Tatar woman and, up until mid-January, had shown no sign of giving in. I have already commented on her steadfastness and stoicism. She has had no news of her husband for a long time now, nor any letters from him. She has never once complained about her fate. Now she has aged, her face has grown shadowed, she has lost her good looks, and she is not yet thirty. She was evidently quite good-looking in her younger days. Supple, slender, with a natural intelligence and tact, she was no doubt a beautiful and desirable young woman when she was between seventeen and twenty. And, when even younger, she would probably have put you in mind of that unforgettable image of a young Tatar girl, portrayed by Leo Tolstoy in *A Captive in the Caucasus*. With her three children, Faina's life had not turned out to be an easy one as it was, but nowadays it has become totally difficult; she can barely cope with both her family and her work. Her mother-in-law lives with her, an old woman who is more or less a child herself and needs looking after. Faina dreams of being evacuated, of leaving with her children to return to her origins, in the Penzenskaya region. But, since August, every attempt at evacuation has failed. Now Faina, like all of us, is living through particularly hard times. Her robust nature has held out so far, but will it continue to hold out now?

Andreyev, who also has aged and developed dark shadows, has found the strength and the willpower within himself to overcome all obstacles. When my wife happened to call in at the Archives on an errand for me, she came upon this domestic scene illustrating our new way of life there.

A conversation between my wife and Andreyev abruptly switched to the topic of public toilets. 'For a kilo of bread I would go and clean the public toilets,' said Andreyev, 'but for the moment I have enough to do taking out all the shit from our apartment morning and evening.'

'We don't take out all of ours,' my wife remarked.

'Do you mean to say that the toilets are actually working at your place?'

'No, they're not, but in the south, you know, they feed their stoves with pressed dung, so we are burning it too.'

There you have an absolutely modern conversation, if not quite one for the drawing room.

4 February 1942. The 228th day of the war. Yet another day of war. I know nothing of what is going on in the outside world. The crumbs of news that are being reported in the newspapers and over the radio do nothing, in fact, to clarify what is happening in the world. 'We occupied point L., we surrendered point B., the spoils of war were such and such…' They don't actually say anything.

Where is mankind heading? How will this most brutal carnage end? When will it end? Dreadful questions! And perhaps superfluous now as well, given the utter impossibility of answering them in any way; of foreseeing to even a limited extent how they might eventually be resolved. The war will undoubtedly last several years more, and here in Leningrad we have not even held out for six months yet!

Should I continue with my notes, now that my small world has become even more restricted? I have made up my mind to do so. My faraway friend, when reading these notes, will discard or skip whatever he finds uninteresting or unnecessary. And I can't tell exactly what will be needed and what will not.

For instance, the going price of a man's suit is about one and a half or two kilos of bread. By the way, a neighbour who had exchanged a suit in this way for a quarter of a bread ration card, shouted from the rooftops that she had lost the card, so as not to have to share it with her son or her aunt.

Even when they do manage to inter a dead body in a cemetery, not everyone has the benefit of an individual burial, that is, of being given a separate grave. People are laid out in trenches, so that nowadays you often hear: 'It wouldn't be good to land in a trench.' Or: 'Watch out, or you'll end up in a trench.'

That one was for a language specialist. Here is one for a stage producer. A crowd of people in the street. All are very poorly dressed, but there are nevertheless some women who are trying to appear 'chic' by allowing to peep out from under their skirts the now accepted baggy oriental trousers in red, brown or even light blue. There are others who simply go around without skirts, with just thick knickers as their lower garment. Headscarves are often worn in the place of other headgear. Both men and women often cover their mouths and noses with a scarf or a band of white cloth. Felt boots are by far the most common form of footwear, sometimes worn down to an incredible extent. There still remain some 'ladies' in shabby astrakhan or moth-eaten squirrel fur coats, so popular in recent years. There are many 'dry-land sailors' strolling along the embankment, who are actually civilians dressed in naval uniform. There are some women in naval uniform too, and it suits them extremely well.

For a touch of local colour, I should also add the example of Yevgenia Alexandrovna Tolmacheva-Karpinskaya, who goes around in ankle-length skirts whose hems drag along the ground, such as were fashionable for women some forty years ago. And on her head she wears a perennial beret of about the same vintage.

8 February 1942. The 232nd day of the war. I am in a frantic hurry to live… At my side is that marvellous, rare creature, my wife and friend. Today is her birthday.

She is not getting enough to eat. She gathers a few things

together and takes them to the marketplace to barter. She flared up at me again. She broke out into red blotches when I ventured to doubt whether, in her weakened state and with a cold already, it would actually be expedient – going by my theory of what constitutes an 'intelligent economy' – for her to be standing at the marketplace in the cold wind. She might well manage to get some bread or cereal, but it could be at the cost of taking to her bed completely. We spoke to one another in a state of nervous tension, straining every nerve to hold ourselves in check.

This is how people lose their reason. Whether they are then behaving reasonably or unreasonably, it would be a bit difficult to say! So now my wife has gone off to the marketplace, and I have taken off my belt, held in readiness for a long time, and have measured it... Like that, just in case.

My wife has returned. She has come back with 100 grams of bread in exchange for a dress. And she is happy. Her eyes have regained their sparkle. And I feel better now that things have improved for her, but I feel worse, even sadder, because of my awareness of what we, our state of mind, our mood, our relationship, depend upon. Upon 100 grams of bread!

Yesterday my wife and I had an unsettling experience. Valya, the little girl we had wanted to look after, came to our apartment. We were at work, so she went round to our neighbours. She explained to them that she was starving, that she had grown weak and had no strength left, and had come to spend the night with us. We are living in the hallway nowadays, and we don't have so much as a square metre spare in which another person could stretch out. Valya had really let herself go: she hadn't washed for several months, she was black with filth, her hair was stuck together in clumps, she was infested with lice, her gaze was lacklustre and her face was swollen from drinking too much water. While she was round at the neighbours', she fell off her chair.

What were we supposed to do? My wife announced firmly that we had nowhere for anyone to stay overnight. Then Valya announced that she did not have the strength to go home; that she had come on a particular errand. She and her mother were to be evacuated, and were in need of money, belongings, food! She had not brought her bread ration card with her. We felt obliged to feed her and to give her some money, although nowhere near the amount she was asking (600 – 700 roubles). At first my wife gave her fifty roubles, but she asked for another twenty. My wife suggested taking her home on a sled, but it turned out that her mother had had to go somewhere, so Valya could not have gone home in any case. She spent the night with the neighbours. She said that all their belongings had been either sold or bartered, and that anything left had been burnt. I was sorry to see that she was not wearing the overcoat that my wife had given her, in spite of the bitter cold. The overcoat had not been burnt, but it was not clear what had become of it either.

My wife and I were overcome by terrible depression and indecision. What could we do? To take her in would mean accelerating our own end and, basically, would solve nothing. To give her our last crust, our money... Our conscience demanded a clear and honest decision. We could do no more than give her what we already had done. This morning she left. I didn't even see her go.

I have never been able to come to terms with the idea of mere existence, of being nothing more than a living creature, any more than I could accept the opposite extreme – to provide future manure. There are still many unresolved issues here, particularly nowadays, when tens of millions of human lives must be lost, in order that the nations to which they belong by birth shall live. All my life I have grappled with questions about God and about nature. I have to confess that all these questions have simply remained unanswered. It is true that I am not a believer. But it would be even more true to say that I have held myself aloof from solving such issues. They are beyond me. I only know that there is no God managing the world in accordance with the laws of love. And I don't know, and don't want to know, about any other gods. I am the god for myself... As for a god identified with nature, the self-creation of nature is not a concept that I find comprehensible. The universe is too immense, its laws are too mighty and too complex, the genesis of life is such an enigma, the construction of a living body is so intricate, and the irrationality of nature so terrifying. Quite often I find nature incompatible with my human intellect. As far as I am concerned, nature is incomprehensible. Particularly now, in these dreadful years and these days of the human slaughter of other intelligent beings. I bow before the grandeur and the beauty of nature, but I also shudder at nature's cruelty, blindness and irrationality.

10 February 1942. The 234th day of the war. A snowy February day. Spasmodic gunfire. People passing by. Little sleds. Dead bodies. Brown stains on the snow. Collapsed columns by the shop doorways. Sheets of plywood instead of glass in the building windows. The wrecked chassis of a lorry opposite the Sphinxes. A pillar festooned with old posters, left over from the summer. A glass showcase fixed to the University railings, with the latest official news bulletin dated 1 November and some extremely outdated cartoons. A clock showing an unreal time. And all this on my way to work.

In a matter of days the second evacuation of the Academy staff is due to take place. Everyone who can leave is doing so! 'Let Petersburg become a wilderness again!' Can it be that this ancient and dreadful prophesy is about to come true?

It is night time now. Somewhere, and evidently somewhere not so far away from us, heavy shells are falling. Somewhere the earth would gasp, sigh at the shock, and the walls of the building would start to move, to vibrate. Then a tense silence once more. I can't hear the gunfire in this windowless hallway where we live nowadays.

And, during these tense moments when one random hit would be enough to ensure that nothing remained of these pages, our home, most likely of our whole building, I am writing a poem. Wrapped up in my work, I am not paying much attention to the eerie stillness of the night, interrupted by deafening explosions and the quivering of the building walls.

We are living on our nerves. Because of their starving or semi-starved condition, many people have sunk into a torpor or become stupefied. Others lose their self-control, become irritated, quarrelsome. You have to go on living somehow, show some indications of life. It is much better to write a poem than to curse everyone and everything or to torment yourself because of your impotence to put right any of what is going on around you, to change anything in your life.

It is not difficult to die, but it is extremely hard to be dying…

19

900,000 Are Leaving

Kniazev's diary continues:

20 February 1942. The 244th day of the war. The inhabitants of our ill-starred city are abandoning all their belongings, their homes – where they did at least have a roof over their heads – and their loved ones who, if they are in a weak condition, are being left behind to die, and they are turning their backs on Leningrad. They are arriving in droves at the Finland railway station, young and old, men and women, dragging their goods and chattels on little sleds, just a few packages per person. An almighty exodus. And those who are staying behind clamp their jaws shut and keep silent. In their eyes there is anxiety and hidden anguish. Though there are some who, on the contrary, appear completely indifferent. What will be, will be!

I am performing my duty as a chronicler of everyday life. I stare into each face, every pair of eyes of those that I encounter. I am trying to notice everything, write down everything that I can see within my own small world. At the moment I am faced with the task of preparing my handwritten and typed materials for trans-mission to the Archives of the Academy of Sciences. I would also like to commit to paper some of the literary ideas that have come to me over time, fragments of recollections shedding light on the past. In brief, to sum things up.

'As long as the Archives of the Academy of Sciences remain intact, your manuscripts will be perfectly safe,' I assured one of the research professors who was being evacuated with the University.

I need to speed up the process of putting my manuscripts and papers in order, too. The cold prevents me from working in my study; in the hole where I exist at the moment, there isn't room to swing a cat. With rare exceptions, my writings are materials known to no one, never published. At the present time, when so many materials and cultural memorabilia of especial value are being destroyed, even documents of lesser importance assume significance. That being so, perhaps my manuscripts too deserve protecting and preserving. In January I put the finishing touches to a framework within which all my papers can be put into order, and I made the decision to transfer them to the Archives of the Academy of Sciences for their temporary or, in the event of my death, their permanent safekeeping. Assuming the Archives themselves survive!

Right now all my thoughts are focused on how to keep alight the dwindling flame of life in the Archives for which I am responsible, and to maintain them as one of the most significant sets of archives recording the history of Russian culture and of its science in particular, compiled over two centuries and more.

My colleagues and I are increasingly running out of strength...

22 February 1942. The 246th day of the war. My wife is getting thinner, not by the day but by the hour. At the moment she is at the food distribution centre, where she is supposed to be given a piece of meat. She left early this morning, having had nothing to eat. Yesterday she was on the go from morning till night, running to the marketplace to barter something, then to the canteen to fetch some porridge. I am afraid that her strength will fail her. Will mine? I am holding out. But sometimes I lose my strength entirely.

A young woman dropped by, one of the students. She has only three exams to go before graduating from the University. She is not willing to be evacuated with the University, so they have crossed her off the list. There is a lot of nervous tension at the University: to go, or not to go? She is not going on account of her mother, for whom the journey itself would be an insuperable ordeal. It wouldn't be better there, it won't be worse here. 'There we would be refugees, here we have a roof over our heads and one or two things that we could barter.' Her two aunts, her mother and she herself are fighting tooth and nail to cling on to life. Her grandfather, Alexander Petrovich Karpinsky, instilled in them a great zest for life, a will to survive.

'My initial horror has given way to anger,' she told me. 'If I survive the war and reach the age of fifty or so, I intend to write my memoirs. I will write down everything that people will tend to forget, or be reluctant to remember. No one is writing down anything at the moment, you know: the time isn't right, and those who are running away from Leningrad will have only their own stories to tell. Which is why I am trying to remember everything, so as to be able to write it down later on.'

Naturally, I didn't breathe a word about how, at precisely this moment, I am writing down everything that I see, that I think and experience. Immediately, spontaneously, without worrying about any contradictions, long-windedness or repetitions. Because such is real life. And what will be written later on, in the form of memoirs, will be a far cry from what we are living through now.

Three heavy naval cannon have been installed right by the bridge, at an angle to our building. There is a great deal of military traffic along the embankment again, reminiscent of September. There was shelling going on the whole time I was riding to work. The shells were exploding somewhere in the vicinity of Nevsky Prospect and Sadovaya Street.

Everything I saw made a very weighty impression on me. Daunting ordeals lie ahead of us. Today my wife's frail body and strained nervous system were unable to hold out any longer: she burst into tears. I look at her with a secret, hidden fear: her face has become shadowed, hollow-cheeked. Yesterday she complained of pain in her lower gums. Today, even early in the morning, she was very weak when she got up, but now she is working: she has fetched firewood from the basement to our third floor, has lit the stove and put less than half a pound of dried peas on to boil, to last the two of us for two days – all we have left of our rations until the end of the first ten-day period next month. 'I'm sorry, I don't think I can last out,' my wife said to me in a low and humble voice. And tears, big tears, rolled down the little, wrinkled old lady's (!) face of my utterly stoical wife and companion.

And it is quite possible that we won't last out! At work today I asked how we could help L.V. Modzalevsky. It turned out that he was beyond help! His wife is on the verge of slipping away, and he is most likely doomed too. It is dreadful to be thinking about this like an outsider.

Our life is becoming more difficult by the hour. Everyone who can is hurrying to get out of the city. And what lies ahead? 'Ahead,' says my wife, 'lies utter hopelessness.' I try to comfort her. I get a grip on myself. I take up a book of poetry. I lose myself in it. 'You look at life philosophically,' my wife tells me, 'but I simply love it. Do you understand? I truly love life.'

In the afternoon the sun shone blindingly on the white mantle draped over the Neva and its embankments, covered all over with a fresh fall of snow. I rode along, shading my face from the dazzling sun, and I thought: 'I still have this, the present moment. It exists! And there's no need to dwell on the future!'

But at work I let nothing show. I was cheerful, animated. I spoke to Andreyev, who has a doctorate in history, and who was cooking something on the stove. I tried to organize some resumption of work in the Archives. As usual, ashes were flying out of the stove from the files we were burning; in front of me sat dismal, tired, hungry people – it made my heart ache.

At home it is cold and chaotic, but the very worst aspect is the hopelessness of our existence. But I'm not giving in yet!

There has been so much to occupy my thoughts during these past days. I have written down a great deal of it, but not all. Naturally, my notes will need careful editing. But what I have wanted to achieve so far has been to convey at least a part of my thoughts and experiences, even if my writing lacks system and consistency of style. There is some justification for my haste.

On the pavement today I had to give way to two sleds tied together coming from the opposite direction. On them lay a corpse, carefully and lovingly sewn into a sky-blue plush velvet coverlet. And for some unknown reason, I gave a kind of shudder. Why? It was, after all, a thoroughly typical scene for Leningrad these days. Other passers-by did not so much as bat an eyelid! Was it an excess of nervous tension, over-sensitivity? Well, call it what you will. I shuddered. Precisely because of that sky-blue plush velvet coverlet. I had gazed dispassionately at many corpses wrapped in canvas or old cloth. But at that moment the blue of the coverlet was so bright in the frosty sunlight that it was stamped on my gaze in the same way that the blue expanse beyond the sun was blinding my eyes.

This encounter took place near the University, that deserted, abandoned old building so dear to my heart. And thus, deep in thought, I rode up to the Academy of Arts, likewise deserted and abandoned. There was snow piled in front of the locked main entrance, on which someone had left the dark-brown traces of defecation. Opposite it were the Sphinxes, my constant companions during these twelve and a half years of my life. There were heaps of snow around them. And they were deep in snow themselves. But they remain, so far they remain! And I grew calm. They speak to me of the 3,500 years of the pre-history of mankind. The real history of mankind still lies ahead!

20

A Cold and Uncomfortable Journey

Lidiya Okhapkina had already lost all hope of getting out of Leningrad when, on 4 March 1942, the very same lieutenant who had brought the parcel from her husband, turned up on her doorstep and asked her to make preparations for a rapid departure:

We would be crossing Lake Ladoga by lorry. In order to do this I had to apply to the District Executive Committee for the travel documents, and then go to Tchaikovsky Street to collect a parcel. I was so happy, so very happy! That same day I went to the Executive Committee for the Vasilievsky Island district to apply for the documents there. They warned me that the route was dangerous; that there had been instances where vehicles had fallen through the ice. The main thing, they added, was that we had to take full responsibility for the journey. This seemed to me a ridiculous thing to say and I asked them: 'And if we die of hunger here, will you take full responsibility for that?' No, I will go, no matter what has been happening there. The next morning I went to fetch the parcel, after I had fed the children and given them a kiss. I took a sled and went first of all to my husband's older brother's, to pick up a suitcase in which there were a few things belonging to me, such as a suit of my husband's and my coat for autumn. He lived in First Red Army Street, again quite a long way away. I got there without any particular incidents. As usual, the city was gloomy and grey, snowdrifts everywhere. But the sun began to shine and its rays glanced off both the houses and the people's faces. It seemed to me as though there was the beginning of something a bit more cheerful in their eyes. Besides, in February, they had increased the bread ration for both the children and me by fifty grams. Having retrieved my suitcase from my in-laws, I suggested that they should accompany me. I promised to share whatever was in the parcel with them. I still hadn't got it. They refused. They too looked emaciated. I crossed the whole of the city again to get to Tchaikovsky Street, to pick up the parcel. Along the way I stopped in for some bread and I ate it all, because I was hoping that there would be something for the children to eat in the parcel. The whole time I was uneasy because of the children. Since they were on their own there, with nothing to eat, they were probably lying on their beds and crying. By then it was beginning to get dark; it was eight in the evening. When I had dealt with all the paperwork and taken the parcel, I went home. It was truly quite a walk!

When I finally reached home, it was already three o'clock in the morning. I didn't have the strength to drag the sled over the high threshold of the entryway. I left everything in the street and, almost on all fours, climbed the stairs until I reached our door. I opened it and called out for Rosa, looking in on her for an instant. The children, hearing my voice, both began to cry. Ah, my darlings, you are alive! Now I will feed you! Rosa and I went down the stairs at full pelt. I said to her: 'Hurry, the sled is standing there outside the entrance! Hurry! There's plenty to eat there – I will stuff you full of food! With a great deal of effort we dragged all the luggage indoors. I undressed and fell on the bed, exhausted. The children were crying, but for twenty minutes I was in no state to go to them. Then I opened the parcel. There turned out to be almost nothing but dried rye bread and just two packets of millet in it. We quickly lit the stove and put on some porridge to cook. I fed the children and Rosa. I was getting things ready all night long. I was in no condition to move either hand or foot. Rosa summoned a couple of women to help me, and I gave them some of the dried bread.

The next day, 6 March 1942, I set off once more for Tchaikovsky Street, with the children and the luggage. The assembly point was there. A woman offered to help me transport

181

the belongings, while I had the children. I had already given her half a kilo of millet and four pieces of dried rye bread. It was eleven o'clock and the time of assembly had been set for twelve noon. She was debilitated just like me, and was hauling the sled along with considerable difficulty. We were both barely making any headway. Neither of us had any strength. I was in a highly nervous state, afraid that we would be late. There was a snowstorm sweeping along the street, whipped by a fierce wind. The time was already half-past one and we were only just coming up to the Liteiny Bridge. You were allowed to go that way in the daytime. What if we were too late? All my torments, the squandering of my last reserves of energy would have been in vain. By then I had shared out almost all the dried bread, the cereal too. Which meant we would go hungry again. Such thoughts were enough to break my heart. My head was thudding. I was soaked in sweat again. I had put on clean linen for the journey, two woollen dresses and my husband's suit on top of them for warmth and safe keeping. I had become too hot. I unbuttoned my overcoat. The wind scoured my face, but I felt nothing. One last effort, one more step, one more... I started counting steps again. From this journey, from this biting wind, I later caught a chill and it turned into raging pleurisy, with a high fever, but I'll keep that for later.

When we finally got there, it was three o'clock. A lorry was standing there – it hadn't gone. Apparently there were other late-comers, not just me. When I had found somewhere to sit in the lorry, they warned me again that the journey would be dangerous. We would come under fire, and so forth. I said that I was aware of that, but I was going just the same. As we travelled through the city, I mentally made my farewells: 'Goodbye, my long-suffering city,' I thought. 'Goodbye to all the people I know.'

There was a snowstorm sweeping over the lake too, but not a severe one. To start with, we kept up a good pace, then we went absolutely slowly. A man was moving ahead of us, inspecting the road and pushing aside the snow with his skis, because they were afraid of holes left by the shells, where the ice was thin.

And so along this road I went, in a snowstorm, on a lorry, with my baby daughter and my son. There were ten or twelve of us making the journey. Just women and children. The driver was a soldier, and there was another man sitting in the cab with him.

I was the weakest of them all. It seemed to me that we had been travelling for an eternity. The lorry had been boarded over with plywood and a certain amount of exhaust gas had built up inside it. My head was spinning and aching. Both the children and I drifted into a state of semi-consciousness. I felt sick and vomited several times. I felt shivery. I could sense that I was running a high temperature. I was absolutely burning up. Someone gave me some kind of medicine. They put a damp towel on my head. I became indifferent to everything, I drifted in and out of consciousness. When I came to, I asked where I was, where the children were. They told me that I was there in the lorry, that my children were alive. Someone had given them something to eat, someone had put them on the potty. I cannot imagine how I managed to survive that journey. I was weakened by hunger, by the strains and stresses of the move and, on top of that, I had caught a chill and was running a high temperature. Probably it was the maternal instinct, making me fight for the lives of my children – to the last breath, as they say.

The first stop. The first evacuation point. Good, kind-hearted people were there to receive us. They helped us down from the lorry, handed down the children. They laid me on a bench.

A big shed had been constructed out of new planks. Benches lined the walls. There were two or three cast-iron stoves in the middle, which were kept constantly burning. They brought us something to eat. They fed the children on semolina with condensed milk. They brought me some meat broth with noodles, but I couldn't eat any of it. My whole mouth and throat were furred with something and felt rough. I couldn't swallow and I had also lost my appetite. I gave my meal to the driver. The next day we travelled on again. We were supposed to get as far as the city of Cherepovets. My husband's military unit was stationed there for a while. We stopped again along the way in a village belonging to the Leningradskaya region. Almost the entire village had been burnt down by the Germans. We all spent the night in one of the houses that had remained intact. I felt extremely unwell and had a dreadful cough. The fever stayed high all the time. But they gave me some aspirin belonging to one of the other women. After that there was one more stop in Tikhvin. This town had been almost totally destroyed.

Eventually, on 11 March 1942, we reached the city of Cherepovets. When the lorry stopped outside a house, my husband immediately leapt on board. He looked all around, then jumped off again. He hadn't recognized us, but I recognized him straight away, of course. The emotion of the moment had robbed me of breath, and I couldn't call out. The children hadn't recognized him. He was in military uniform. I could hear him asking whether or not I had arrived. They told him that his wife and children were in the lorry. He leapt up again and began to look around. Recognition dawned. He recognized us and said in a hoarse voice: 'Is it you? Is it you?' He jumped down from the lorry again. He burst into tears and for some reason he took off his hat. Then, eventually getting control of himself, he said: 'Lidiya! Tolya!', and his eyes filled with tears again. I couldn't say anything back to him. I looked at him in silence. I had a lump in my throat. I wanted to speak, but my tongue seemed to have been struck dumb. The lorry was crammed full of bundles, and I was sitting right in a corner. Then he called out: 'Tolya, come here to me quickly!' In a voice not my own I said: 'He can't manage to walk.' The sum total of the conversation was exactly as I have narrated it. The meeting was both joyful and sad. It has remained in my memory my whole life. Then he got us out one at a time and carried us to a house. We were four families to be given an empty room. Each family occupied a corner of it.

It was dark in the room. The city of Cherepovets was blacked out at night, too. The husbands were in good shape, but the wives were emaciated. Husbands and wives whispered softly to one another, sobbed quietly. I was unable to talk: my cough got in the way. I was running a fever, my head and chest were hurting. The owner of the house got some milk from somewhere and gave it to me and the children to drink hot. She said that the next day she would be able to provide some more milk and some potatoes. I was so happy. I

184

couldn't believe it. Milk, potatoes – what luck! I decided to change my underwear. When I had undressed, I stood naked in front of my husband. 'See what I have become,' I said. I was nothing but skin and bone. My chest was especially awful – just ribs. And I was a nursing mother when the war began. My legs were skinny, hardly plumper than a half-litre bottle. Vasili looked at me and started to blink his eyes again. 'Never mind,' he said, 'since the bones are in good shape, the body will follow.' There was no possibility of any intimacy between us, it was absolutely out of the question, although we had not seen one another for ten months. We stayed in that room for five days. Then we decided to go on to Saratov. My husband was granted ten days' leave. I had family in Saratov: my mother and two sisters. We boarded a special train coming from Leningrad. It was made up of goods vans. A cold and uncomfortable journey again. The passengers were being evacuated from Leningrad, so they were as thin and worn as I was. Travelling with us was the wife and son of that same lieutenant who had come to our place in Leningrad. And he was there himself. They wanted to go to Saratov with us. During the journey exhausted and ill people died.

They fed us at each stop, and my husband would run into the station with a saucepan in his hand. He would bring back porridge or soup, but I hardly ate anything. I was feeling more and more unwell all the time. At one stop I got out as well, to breathe in some fresh air. My husband was meanwhile feeding the children. Suddenly, without giving any kind of warning whistle, the train began to move off. I made a run for our van, gasping for breath. It wasn't far and I managed to grab hold of a handle. The train began to pick up speed, but my feet, where the snow had been cleared from the platform, did not touch the van. Someone shouted: 'Lidiya is outside!' Before my eyes flashed the face of my husband, the faces of my children, and a thought struck like a bolt of lightning: 'This is where I am destined to die! Not from hunger, not in the bombing, but here and now!' I fainted. Vasili managed to grab me by my coat collar. The lieutenant helped him to haul me inside the van. When I came to, the toes had been ripped off my

185

felt boots. The big toe on my right foot had been crushed, blood was seeping out of it. If my felt boots had not been big for me – they were a larger size; not mine but my husband's – I would probably have lost my feet, at least up to my ankles, if not higher up. If my husband had been even a second later in grabbing me by the collar and dragging me clear of the wheels, the train would have crushed me to death.

After this experience and with my illness to contend with, I collapsed completely. The ceaseless coughing coupled with the high temperature wore me down, and I thought that I would die on the journey. The train made slow progress. At one stop a medical team boarded the train. A doctor made a cursory examination of the people and ordered the very weak and the most ill to be carried out on stretchers. When he took a look at me, he ordered them to take me out too, saying: 'This one to the hospital – spotted fever.' I said that I had already had spotted fever in 1922, when I was a girl, and that I probably had pneumonia. He said: 'We'll sort it out in hospital.'

My skin was dry and peeling off from emaciation, and it had a sort of rash on it. I looked like a plucked chicken. That is what made the doctor think I had typhus. My husband took fright. If I was in the hospital, then where would the children go? We decided that, once the doctor and the medical team had gone, we would quickly get off from the other side of the train, straight into the snow. A woman with her husband and son got off with us. The train moved on and we were left sitting on our luggage in the snow. Our husbands went off to find out where we had stopped and to hire horses and sledges to get us to a railway station. When they came back with the sledges, my husband said that this stop was Semibratovo in the Yaroslavskaya region. We loaded the sledges and set off for the railway station. They laid me on a bench. I could neither move nor stand. We were surrounded by people staring at me. Evidently, my appearance held a particular fascination and dread for them:

'How thin she is and how terrible she looks, and her with an unweaned baby!'

186

'But perhaps it's not hers.'

'Probably she's the baby's grandmother.'

We stopped in one of the villages in the Yaroslavskaya region. For a long time no one could bring themselves to take us in, being afraid of me, thinking that I had an infectious disease. Then one woman took us in. My husband left the following day. He bought a sack of potatoes for us. He obtained half a kilo of real farm butter and some milk. When the time came to say goodbye, he kissed me on the brow. I told him that he had kissed me the way you kiss a corpse. He then kissed me on the lips.

I was ill for a long time. The village doctor came to see me, and he too diagnosed me as having typhus. The owner of the house took fright, and I was removed to a cold and dirty outhouse. I lay there for two days. After that, when the doctor came back again, he gave me a thorough examination, then diagnosed a pulmonary inflammation. I asked him to apply suction cups to me. He came and set them in place. I was ill for more than a month. Then I started to get better. Once I had recovered, I began to work on the collective farm as a farm labourer. I didn't have the strength to work hard enough to earn anything. I bartered all the clothes that I had brought with me to get milk for the children. I had never lived in the country in my life and I didn't know how to work like a peasant, but life taught me. I lived in the village for three years.

21

We Are Still Alive!

Returning to Kniazev's diary:

13 March 1942. The 265th day of the war. There is broth, steaming-hot broth on the table. And we gulp it avidly, lap it up like famished dogs. And beside it is my book – *About Poetry in the Bible* – full of scintillating and pithy ideas, sometimes paradoxical and debatable ones, and my pencil for taking notes. I take from it what I need, lively and vibrant to this day, while the rest, like slag, I leave behind. The broth made from – well, I don't even know what it's made from! – seems to us like the nectar of the gods. It seems to contain the very essence of poetry – this warm steam rising from it.

My wife had brought an extra little piece of bread, for which she had bartered a shirt at the market. How lucky we are to be still living like this! The stove isn't even smoking today. My wife cleared the soot from the stove-pipe.

What more could we need? Only one thing: just a modicum of certainty about tomorrow, or even nearer than that – about this coming evening. It is actually quite unbearable to live like this – in the present moment, in the very instant, without any kind of a future (naturally, I am referring here to our own personal future).

14 March 1942. The 266th day of the war. Nothing in particular. A day like any other. A night like any other in the besieged city. The siege has not been broken, and the whole quality of our existence stems from that. I had made up my mind a long time ago not to think about the future, but now the question presents itself again: what are we to do? For us the decision was irrevocable – to remain in Leningrad and not to go anywhere else. But now the very facts of life raise the issue of leaving Leningrad again. We would not survive next winter – even if we should last until then – in a city in ruins, without firewood. This winter tens, if not hundreds of thousands of people, exhausted from starvation, simply succumbed to the cold and froze to death in their unheated rooms. To await such an eventuality with philosophical detachment would be fruitless. It means that the question of leaving Leningrad must be addressed. But where could we go? And what about the Archives?

And suddenly the future has risen up like a grey wall. The future must be given thought.

I was not able to go to work today because my wheelchair was in need of repair and because, in her debilitated state, my wife was unable to cope today with the combined responsibilities of repairman and chauffeur.

I spent the whole day reading the poetry of Baudelaire, Verlaine, Verhaeren and others.

15 March 1942. The 267th day of the war. Today is my birthday. I have reached the age of fifty-five. I am weary, worn out with hunger and cold, spiritually at rock bottom, crushed by the whirlwind of events, but I am not an old man, I am not soft in the head. I still feel there is sufficient strength in me to put up a struggle and, if need be, to die. What else can I do? I have lived my life. It is true that I did not manage to spend some three or five years in retirement, busying myself with my books, my collections, my unfinished projects. Evil times intervened. The entire world, the whole of our planet has gone up in flames.

I got up early. I got dressed by the stove. What joy it is to warm yourself beside a hot stove in a cold room! It had been banked up for the night and, at the approach of morning, had still not cooled down. Now I am seated at my table. It is true that the room is in a mess and that there is acrid smoke coming from the burning stove that makes your eyes water. But how fortunate I am that I still have my wife with me! She is doing her best to stay cheerful. At the moment she is making the coffee. It doesn't matter that my hands are freezing and that both she and I are wearing our winter overcoats (outdoors it is nineteen degrees below freezing again!), we are nonetheless alive. And she and I love one another.

'Come to me, my dear,' and I gave her a kiss – so frail, so old-looking. And she smiled at me with the full force of her tender and loving gaze, still luminous and clear. 'My joy, my linchpin, my friend, my faithful and joyous wife...' I couldn't continue. I thought to myself: 'Can it really be true that our life is over, that everything is over?' But I drove such thoughts away, drove them right away. I didn't need thoughts like that.

We sat down to drink our coffee. I warmed my wife's hands. On the table lay my copies of Petrarch, Verhaeren, Alexander Blok... So many thoughts, so many images!

But we are still alive!

18 March 1942. The 270th day of the war. Today, at two o'clock in the afternoon, our Vasilievsky Island was unexpectedly subjected to heavy shelling.

I was returning from the Archives along the embankment, immersed in my thoughts. Suddenly the air above the Neva was ripped, like silk. And immediately a rumbling noise started up somewhere. Ahead of me the passers-by had already flattened themselves on the snow. All this was stupefyingly sudden. Only this morning, opening the front door and passing through it, while my wife was getting my wheelchair ready under the porch of our academicians' home, I was thinking how heavenly, how peaceful it was, not to have the guns banging away!

Then out of the blue – a shell whistling over my head, a second, a third... And bang, bang, bang! The explosions were somewhere nearby. Some people were flat on their faces, others running, crouching close to the ground beside the buildings. It was too risky to stay out in the open, so I went in under the gateway of the former Cadet Corps building on the side of the embankment. A sentry let me in. I spent thirty to forty minutes there, while the shelling was going on. But I went back out onto the embankment

190

without waiting for the full restoration of calm. Academician Krachkovsky was standing under the porch of the former Menshikov Palace. White-faced, tense, silent and haughty. The shelling intensified once more. He took a few steps with me in silence, then came to a standstill again, but by then we were in an angle of the building.

My wife meanwhile was sitting in the canteen in the basement of the Zoological Museum. I felt relatively tranquil on her account. Mistakenly, as it transpired. One of the shells fell precisely between the Otto Hospital and the Academy canteen. With a deafening crash the shock wave shattered all its windows. And my wife was sitting beside one of the windows but, by a stroke of luck, the shrapnel or shell fragments and the shards of glass flew above her head without hitting her, although the dreadful noise of the explosion made her right ear go deaf. The whole place was in chaos. My wife's first thought was for what might have happened to me. I was riding along the embankment, you see, directly under the shellfire. But, fortunately, she did not come out. She stayed there and waited and was even given food, which they had stopped serving during the height of the confusion.

31 March 1942. The 283rd day of the war. With what love, what tenderness I was looking today at my collection of art, at the extracts from my history of culture, at the various literary ventures begun or simply contemplated. All it lacked was a few years, you know, just three little years!

My wife approached me and smilingly asked if I was still writing. She reminded me of a story in which a happy man is enthusiastically putting pen to paper, inspired by his good fortune in being able to write what he wanted and in what manner he pleased. But when they took a close look at what he was writing, it turned out not to be writing at all – just lines of hooks and loops, not resembling real letters, or simply crossed-out lines. The fortunate fellow was just blissfully happy that he had time enough to be able to write to his heart's content...

We burst out laughing.

'You'd better keep an eye on me!' I told my wife. And we laughed again. It is so rare nowadays for people to laugh.

'Do you think we'll hold out?' she asked me.

'We'll hold out in April and May, and in June. In June or July, we'll get out.'

'And if we don't manage to get out?'

Neither of us spoke.

22

Leningrad Will Never Die

Kniazev's diary continues:

9 April 1942. The 292nd day of the war. I am making haste to live! I woke up early this morning and my mind began to whirl. I must do this, finish that, manage in a few months to accomplish, if only partially, what even three years would have been too little for!

And there is much that I want to write about. I would like to write verses and poems in praise of woman, as wife and companion. In praise of the wives who struggled and survived, but who mostly lost their husbands just the same — men like the astronomer Berg, the archaeologist Chayev, and many others — including that simple-hearted woman who recounted to me the last hours of her husband, Blokhin, the porter at Central Archives.

Perhaps a future poet whose gaze might fall on these scribbled pages of mine will find inspiration in them and will compose verses or a poem in praise of a wife who bore all burdens wholeheartedly and selflessly and supported her husband with all her might... The fact that I am still alive I owe entirely to my wife. Without the need for any fine words, what a selfless worker and modest heroine she is!

13 April 1942. The 296th day of the war. Someone once said: 'Man spreads himself too broadly: it would do no harm to clip his wings a bit.' All this winter I have been living only in the present moment; but at the same time I have also been living in long-ago centuries and millennia, creating a chronological framework for a history of civilization: *The Milestones of Civilization and its Bloodstained Reverses*. What an immense range of possibilities there are in man: soaring flights and plunging falls; geniuses like cosmic stars of the greatest magnitude, and monsters, depraved wretches; those whose names are known to history and billions of those obscure people, unknown to anyone, who could never be remembered by anyone since nothing is known about them, but who lived and died, and who basically make up the human race!

12 May 1942. The 325th day of the war. It turns out that I have a contemporary who is keeping a record of rumours. As I have already mentioned, I have kept no note of them, I have taken only the facts. I only noted down a rumour when it related to a fact that I was unable to verify myself. The contemporary in question is E.G. Oldenburg.

Today she helped me to take down from the wall of our building a poster inscribed with a slogan about the defence of our native city. This poster had been hanging there the whole winter, exposed to the rain, the snow, the blizzards and the shelling. It said: 'We will never surrender our native city!' The Leningraders have stood by their city. In a few years' time – 50 to 100 years, say – this poster will be the pride of some museum. Those who come after us will bow their heads before it. This tattered sheet, carefully preserved, will tell the story of what Leningrad went through better than hundreds of pages of print. It is a living document of our time.

And when E.G. Oldenburg was helping me to remove this poster from the wall, she also told me that she had filled several exercise books, noting all her impressions day after day, and also everything that she heard; rumours.

So, I am not the only one who is writing. But no one else writes the same way as I do. We each see and experience everything in our own way, not all alike.

I found out that during the course of the winter months, out of the 200 residents in our building, sixty-five had died, which is about 35 per cent.

18 May 1942. The 331st day of the war. A wonderful day today. Along the embankment they are hoeing the flower beds, the same ones that I wrote about in the autumn with such hopeless sadness. I didn't think that I would live to see the day when flowers would bloom again in those beds. How moved I was by this long stretch of black earth being prepared for the planting of flowers!

In the Rumiantsev Garden the residents of Vasilievsky Island have laid out a vegetable plot. They have divided the garden into separate sections. Unfortunately, a lot of space is taken up by the slit trenches.

It is hot in the sunshine. To be able to sit and warm yourself, to take pleasure in life! I want so much to live now, to think, to create!

Today, after an interval of six months, I was able to work in my own room again, at my own writing table – and I never believed this would happen...

6 July 1942. The 380th day of the war. The city is rife with rumours. They are disturbing for all of us. Everyone is expecting a German offensive against Leningrad, the total encirclement of the city and all the horrors of a new siege strangling the life out of the Leningraders.

Women with their children pass by in the streets, people transport their bags and baggage in children's prams. They are being moved out compulsorily. A doctor living in our apartment building has sent his wife and two children to Bashkiria. Drenched in sweat, crimson-red, he trundled their bundled-up belongings in a little handcart, while the mother, with one child in her arms and the other clinging to her skirts, walked along with stumbling, weary footsteps.

The lists of those to be evacuated are being compiled by the various organizations. Scholars are bringing their manuscripts to us at the Archives.

I have gathered all my reserves of strength together and, as best I can, am now looking the future calmly in the eye.

I was told about a telegram received from our cleaner Faina, the wife of our boilerman Urmancheiev, the mother of his three children, which said that she had reached home but that, out of the three children, only one had reached the destination with her: two had died on the journey.

My beloved native city, where I am familiar not only with the streets, the squares and the buildings, but also with each pebble! What have they done to it!

'Here is the Nevsky Prospect, here is Morskaya Street,' I wrote during the days of the first siege, at the time of the Civil War, stricken by the defeat and ruin of the city, turned into a wasteland. Except that packs of dogs could be seen in the streets then, rushing headlong somewhere, even along the Nevsky, when the flow of pedestrians dried up towards evening. Nowadays there is not so much as a single dog in the streets...

And here, once more, is the Nevsky, here is Morskaya Street. A terrible bomb crater has sliced off a whole corner of the former Malaya Morskaya Street, now Gogol Street, destroying everything from roof to cellar. The shops are no longer trading, their windows boarded up; floors or whole buildings are uninhabitable, victims of the shelling. The city is once more in ruins. I am living through exactly the same thing for the second time. And today, just like twenty years or more ago, I was in a daze, almost in despair. I calmed myself down – the city recovered from that disaster and will recover now too! My native city will live and flourish. The dreadful days of war will pass, but the city will remain. We ourselves will die, but the city will remain. The city of Peter and of Lenin, both native Russian men of genius, will never die. Through Petersburg, Peter linked Russia with Europe and Lenin drew Europe and the whole world towards the Soviet Union. Leningrad was resurrected before and will be resurrected again, once this war has ended.

There is one issue that I am having to face all the time – whether or not I have the right to abandon the Archives, or 'my ship', as I call it. If it were doomed to destruction, then I would want to go down with it. If I were to leave like this, I would be abandoning the Archives.

'They have ordered you to do so,' a colleague told me, 'and you are duty-bound to obey.'

I requested permission to have until Monday to mull over my reply. But what will my reply be? Agonizing question! I put it to my wife. She gave me her reply in writing. She was candid and clear. So then, we leave! I walked around the Archives as though I had been hit on the head with an axe. Do I have the right to abandon the Archives? Wouldn't I look like a deserter?

My native city, even I am being compelled to abandon you! I should have been getting ready today, but, pencil in hand, I am filling page after page with my writing. I do not wish to be reproached for failing in my duty, for failing to write down all that I saw, heard, read and experienced during the days when my wonderful city was under siege. I am fulfilling my duty to the best of my ability. I am carrying away with me a briefcase full of notes about the wartime days in Leningrad.

11 August 1942. The 416th day of the war. My last day in Leningrad.

I have said my farewells to the city. I have said my farewells to the Sphinxes. The embankment is deserted. On my way from our house to the Archives, I encountered no more than three people – a soldier and two women carrying a coffin on their shoulders. At work I did the rounds of the storage rooms with a feeling of deep distress. Am I leaving them for a while, or for ever? At home confusion reigns. As usual, there are many things still not ready. Four o'clock. At seven o'clock a bus will come to collect our belongings and ourselves.

23

Epilogue

So ended the daily notes of Georgi Kniazev from the besieged city of Leningrad. Then followed the trials and tribulations of evacuation for the wheelchair-bound *blokadnik* and his devoted wife. Their life continued to be hard but, when the siege was lifted, they were able to return to their apartment in Leningrad and pick up the pieces of their former lives. Kniazev resumed his research and administrative work at the Archives and lived until the 1960s when he died at home, in the building on the banks of the Neva which bore memorial plaques to twenty-seven outstanding Leningraders.

The story of Lidiya Okhapkina is one of a mother intent only on saving the lives of her children. Some people might say that there was nothing exceptional, nothing heroic in her story; she did what she had to for the sake of her family. This may be true. Many mothers struggled to keep their children alive during this terrible time but not all succeeded. Sadly Lidiya's joy at having saved her children was short-lived as her tiny daughter Ninochka did not survive, succumbing to a stomach disease and tuberculosis soon after being evacuated from Leningrad.

When reading Lidiya Okhapkina's notes, one can't help thinking how love and starvation clashed with one another in the life of her family. As the saying goes, 'love and hunger rule the world'. Love, it is supposed, can conquer all adversities but even Lidiya's fierce maternal love wasn't enough to save little Ninochka. Had they remained in Leningrad, of course, all three Okhapkins could, and probably would, have died of starvation but nothing could have broken Lidiya's maternal love.

While thinking about Lidiya Okhapkina, we compared her with Yura Riabinkin and Georgi Kniazev. We tried to define what was the driving force in each of these three people during these exceptional times. It seemed to us that for Yura Riabinkin it was his conscience; for Georgi Alexeievich Kniazev it was his intellect and spirit and for Lidiya Okhapkina it was love. This is, of course, a simplification. They were very different people living through complicated, onerous times but, to us, it was these qualities that shone through their notes and diaries. Interestingly these three remarkable characters personified the most basic elements of human existence.

We had already finished translating this book when we came across the actual diary of Yura Riabinkin. Until then we had used the typescript given to us by the editor-in-chief of a Leningrad newspaper. At last we were able to see the actual diary, written in beautiful fluent handwriting; violet ink in a black, cloth-bound notebook. Towards the end of the diary the spaces between the lines became smaller as Yura tried to make his notebook last. The diary began on 22 June 1941; the final entry was made on 6 January 1942. It looked mysterious and strange – the last page, the last entry – and Yura Riabinkin's life was over.

It seemed that Yura's premonition had proved to be correct but we wanted to find out more about this young man to whom we had become very attached while working on his diary. Even when he was suffering the effects of dystrophy and his emotions were in turmoil he wrote in a neat hand and was remarkably clear thinking. What had happened to him, his mother and his sister Ira? The building in which the family had lived had long since been taken over by a company and its former residents had all moved away. We began our search for more news of Yura through newspapers and then, with great success, over the radio. We discovered that Ira Riabinkina was alive and that she worked as a teacher of Russian literature in a high school. We contacted her and with some trepidation, given the circumstances, set off to meet her. It turned out that Ira, now Irina Ivanovna was very agitated too. She was a short, slim, fragile woman, nervous almost to the point of being frightened although it was obvious that we were expected in the small cosy flat that she shared with her husband and family. The table had been laid and refreshments had been prepared. Both Irina Ivanovna's husband and her daughter, a student, looked at us warily as if expecting some sort of trouble.

At first, Irina Ivanovna did not want to tell us anything, saying that it was too hard for her to relive the memories and that she did not want anything to be written about her or her brother. We gently pushed her, saying that Yura's life and his diary belonged to history; that publication of the diary would, in a way, be a kind of memorial to him; that it would be of great importance for young readers to get the feeling of a teenager's life under the conditions of the siege. Eventually she started talking:

From Dzerzhinsky Street to the Admiralty – all this was my district, the familiar places of my childhood. Now, I take every opportunity to avoid the area. We lived in the 3rd July Street, number 34, flat 2. Yura was eight years older than me and I was a little girl, which is why we were never really close. The day that war broke out I was in the Yusupovsky Garden, with some other small children. It was a sunny day and I heard someone shouting: 'War, war, Molotov is making a speech.' I had no idea who Molotov was. I remember the crowds gathering around loudspeakers in the street. There was nobody at home. Then Mother arrived. As for Yura, he was out. He was often out with his friends.

We asked if she remembered the neighbours and she told us:

He was the head of a holding company. Anfissa, his wife, died after the war, a neighbour told me. She hadn't been evacuated. He was rarely at home, but I remember her well – a colourful young woman. I don't know whether Yura stayed with them or not...

I wouldn't say every bit of food was given to me. Mother divided the rations, but Yura's share was not enough for him. He said in his diary that Mother was always the first to finish her rations while mine lasted longer, probably because I was so small. I remember how Yura lay with his face to the wall. The conversation was always about evacuation: 'If the Regional Committee... If we are permitted...' And I also remember Mother getting some warm clothes; quilted trousers and a quilted jacket for Yura. They were giving out quilted hats — a kind of pilot's helmet — and she got two, one for herself and one for him. I can remember him now, clad in all this warm clothing with Mother helping him to stand up. I didn't take much notice of this and didn't really bother to watch what was happening but he did manage to stand.

At that time we were living in the kitchen. It was a big kitchen — we had a stove with a brass railing and on one side of it, in a glass container, was water, which we heated when the stove was lit. Beside it there was a big chest, the lid of which could be raised to form a wooden backrest. I have never seen another one like it. It was possible to put anything in it... Yura stood up, leaning against this chest, supporting himself with a stick, but he couldn't walk, couldn't prise himself away from the chest and he stood like that; bent, exhausted... I remember this precisely...

I have always felt guilty, because I was the one to live — I can't help feeling that way... We had a little sled, on it was placed a suitcase, with silverware, a few silver forks and spoons — all our treasures — in it. I remember Yura's collection of postcards with reproductions of the paintings in the Tretiakov Gallery. He had a lot of them, probably close to 100, which we took with us as well. Later, when I was in the children's reception centre, someone begged them from me. Then there were some items of clothing — all this we took with us. And I remember pushing the sled from behind but Yura stayed at home. Mother was unable to get him onto the sled, she just couldn't, and he himself was unable to walk. There was apparently no way of transporting him — I don't know... It was 12 January.

For a long time we travelled on the special train. I remember the goods van. Oh yes, and when we were making our way to the Moscow railway station on foot along the Nevsky, Mother kept turning round to look back, as if expecting him to be there. She kept saying: 'Yura is back there! Yura is back there!' I was in tears naturally. As soon as we boarded the goods van it began to move and we set off for Ladoga. I remember distinctly passing Lake

Ladoga. We reached Vologda and there I was in the railway station… So many years have passed, but I remember it: a bench, Mother and myself on some bundles… When we arrived, each of us was given a soup plate of millet porridge with cubes of meat in it. Two whole plates! Then they gave us some coupons, and Mother fetched a whole loaf of bread, which was later stolen from under her head at night. And at about 6 a.m. the next morning she lay with foam on her lips, her eyes closed. She died on that bench. Her death certificate said: 'Antonina Mikhailovna, forty years old. Cause of death – dystrophy.' We had been travelling constantly for many days, perhaps weeks. Sometimes we stopped for a while but we never stayed anywhere.

After Mother's death I was sent to a children's reception centre, then to an orphanage where I stayed from 11 February 1942 until 1945. Then I came back to Leningrad. It was Tina who fetched me. The orphanage was in the village of Nikitskaya, which is now four hours ride from Vologda but, at that time, it was necessary to walk twenty-one kilometres through woodland. And so in 1945 Aunt Tina, wearing a greatcoat and carrying a rucksack on her back, walked the twenty-one kilometres to fetch me! She got me out of there and back to Leningrad.

A strange thought comes into my head now and then. What if Yura is still alive? If he was evacuated then, with his love for life, even if he had just a tiny chance to survive, he would have survived. But if so, it wouldn't have been too difficult for him to find me after the war. Or did he feel betrayed, when he was left behind?

Thanks to Irina Ivanovna we learned a lot about Yura, even though we haven't learned how he died and how his diary survived. We had wanted to find out the circumstances of Yura's death, but instead we discovered something quite different – Irina Ivanovna's secret hope that Yura was still alive somewhere …

We finished our work with a strange feeling and the question: were we right to have stirred up all these old memories? Should we have tried to bring to life, once more, these people, their hardships and their pain? Many times we asked ourselves this question and slowly became certain that it was something that we had to do. Everything that we have written about really happened and the living must be told about the victims of the siege and about how they lived and died.

Recommended reading

Goure, Leon, *The Siege of Leningrad*, Stanford University Press, 1962

Overy, Richard, *Russian's War*, Penguin, 1997

Pavlov, Dmitri V., *Leningrad 1941: The Blockade*, The University of Chicago, 1965

Werth, Alexander, *Russia At War 1941-1945*, Berrie & Rockliff, London, 1964

Index